The Modern Stand Mixer Cookbook for the New Bride

100 Incredible Recipes for getting the most out of your new stand mixer

Krysten Brantley

The Modern Stand Mixer Cookbook
for the New Bride
100 Incredible Recipes for Getting the Most
Out of Your New Stand Mixer

Published by Fun Food Home, Inc.
Cover photo credit:
belchonock/ Depositphotos.com

Back cover: / All photos - Depositphotos.com
mpessaris, Yulia_Kotina, nata_vkusidey
Anna_Shepulova

Interior photos: All photos - Depositphotos.com
RuthBlack and CreativeFamily p. 3,
mariakarabella p. 4, lenyvavsha p. 5,
RuthBlack p. 12, nata_vkusidey p. 15, Nadianb
p. 18, KrotovDmitrii p. 21, pinkasevich p. 22,
springfield p. 25, Anna_Shepulova p. 26,
belchonock p. 29, Yulia_Kotina p. 31,
elenademyanko p. 35, bhofack2 p. 39, alju
p. 43, Anna_Shepulova p. 44, Anjela30 p. 47,
StephanieFrey p. 49, bhofack2 p. 50,
SouthernLightStudios p. 53, bhofack2 p. 54,
18042011 p. 57, lenyvavsha p. 58,
ezumeimages p. 61, TeriVirbickis p. 62,
SouthernLightStudios p. 66, StephanieFrey
p. 69, baibaz p. 72, bhofack2 p. 76, fahrwasser
p. 79, grafvision p. 82, alex9500 p. 85,
chiociolla p. 87, HandmadePicture p. 90,
NatashaBreen p. 96, bhofack2 p. 99, robynmac
p. 100, Anna_Shepulova p. 103, studio p. 104,
urban_light p. 107, bogdandreava p. 110,
bhofack2 p. 115, HandmadePicture p. 116,
RuthBlack p. 122, rjgrant2 p. 125,
ArenaCreative p. 126 , urban _light p. 129,
galiyahassan p . 132 , 5 seconds p . 136,
Duranphotography 139 , galiyahassan p. 140,
mpessaris p. 143, andyriver p. 146, apolonia
p. 149, bhofack2 p. 152, yekophotostudio
p. 156 , bhofack 2 p. 159 , asimojet p. 162 ,
ajafoto p. 165, Shebeko p. 167, yuliyagontar
p. 173, Odelinde p. 177

Legal Disclaimer

The information contained in this book is the opinion of the author and is based on the author's personal experience and observations. The author does not assume liability whatsoever for the use of or inability to use any or all information contained in this book, and accepts no responsibility for any loss or damages of any kind that may be incurred by the reader as a result of actions arising from the use of information in this book. Use this information at your own risk. The author reserves the right to make any changes he or she deems necessary to future versions of the publication to ensure its accuracy.

INTRODUCTION

First of all, CONGRATULATIONS!

I mean that if you're ***getting*** married, have just ***gotten*** married OR...you just got your very first stand mixer. For many of us, we really don't get started with stand mixers until we're lucky enough to get one through our bridal registry. That's how it was with me, at least. With that in mind, all of the recipes here are to get you going as someone new to cooking with a stand mixer. There's a little of everything here.

I personally got started with the KitchenAid® brand of mixers. Their 4.5 quart mixer is what every recipe in this book has been tested with. If you have another brand you'll just need to read with that in mind. It should only require a few minor tweaks, if any at all.

In these pages, you'll find a diverse selection of recipes to get you comfortable using your stand mixer as your number one kitchen accessory. It highlights the three main attachments that come with most stand mixers, but also features a few samples from some of the additional attachments that you can buy. This recipe selection not only includes baking recipes offered by conventional stand mixer books but also includes recipes for using your mixer to help you prepare main dishes, appetizers, soups, desserts and many others. These recipes are easy to prepare, with step by step directions that are as detailed as possible. Traditional methods of cooking are made easier and faster with your stand mixer.

The recipe selection consists of basic baking recipes such as breads, pies, cakes, cookies, and frostings. It also includes ideas for pasta dishes, burgers and sausage, ice cream, fancy desserts, sauces and condiments. Your stand mixer will change the way you cook and this recipe guide will help you get creative and comfortable with it in your kitchen.

Discover new and convenient ways of preparing daily meals and short cuts that will save you time. For example, did you know you can use your stand mixer to shred cooked chicken breasts for soups and other dishes? Or that you can make homemade whipped cream that is far better than any store-bought variety? This book will give you the confidence to whip up delicious and memorable meals for those you love.

Here's to new beginnings!

TABLE OF CONTENTS

FLAT BEATER RECIPES

DOUGH HOOK RECIPES

WIRE WHIP RECIPES

FOOD GRINDER

FRUIT VEGETABLE STRAINER

CITRUS JUICER

ROTOR SLICER AND SHREDDER ATTACHMENT (RVSA)

SAUSAGE STUFFER

ICE CREAM MAKER

PASTA ROLLER

RAVIOLI MAKER

PASTA PRESS

GRAIN MILL

ASSEMBLING YOUR TILT-HEAD MIXER

To Attach Bowl

1. Turn OFF the stand mixer.
2. Lift or tilt the motor head back and place mixer bowl onto bowl clamping plate, turn clockwise to secure into the stand mixer.

To Remove Bowl

1. Turn OFF the stand mixer using the speed control.
2. Lift the motor head back and remove the mixer bowl by turning counterclockwise.

To Attach Basic Attachments (Flat Beater, Wire Whip, Or Dough Hook)

1. Turn OFF stand mixer using the speed control.
2. Tilt the motor head back and insert choice of beater onto beater shaft.
3. Press upward and turn the attachment to the right to secure it into the motor head.

To Remove Flat Beater, Wire Whip Or Dough Hook

1. Turn OFF by pressing the speed control to OFF.
2. Tilt the stand mixer motor head up. Press the attachment slightly up and rotate to the left. Then allow attachment to slide off the base.

To Lock Motor Head

1. Tilt motor head and push down to make sure that it is completely down.
2. Position the locking lever to LOCK position.
3. Test if already locked properly by trying to lift up the motor head.

To Unlock Motor Head

1. Turn off stand mixer using the control guide.
2. Position lock lever to UNLOCK position and lift up the motor head.

NOTE: Make sure that the stand mixer motor head is always locked when using the stand mixer.

SPEED CONTROL GUIDE

Stir Speed

This speed is used for slow stirring, mashing and combining different ingredients like incorporating wet to dry mixture, or vice versa. It is also used in combining meats with other ingredients and making homemade ice creams.

Speed 2 - (Slow Mixing)

This speed is used for kneading yeasted dough mixtures, slow mixing, mashing ingredients and stirring mixtures slowly. It is used in stirring and mixing mixtures like heavy batters and sticky candy mixtures.

Speed 4 - (Mixing)

This is also the medium speed and the right speed to use in semi-heavy batter mixing like cookie mixtures, folding sugar into meringues and egg whites and combining shortening and sugar. Attachments like the Slicer or Shredder, Food Grinder, Fruit and Vegetable Strainer and Sausage Stuffer also use this speed.

Speed 6 - (Beating)

This is the recommended speed in beating ingredients like finishing the mixing of cake batters and creaming ingredients such as butters and shortening. The Pasta Press and Citrus Juicer are also used with this speed.

Speed 8 - (Fast Beating)

This is appropriate for incorporating air into the mixtures like whipping heavy cream, egg whites and frostings.

Speed 10 - (Fast Whipping)

This speed is used in quickly whipping small amounts of cream and egg whites and can also be used with the Grain Mill and Pasta attachments.

STAND MIXER ATTACHMENTS AND USE

Your stand mixer comes with 3 basic attachments; the flat edge beater, the wire whip and the dough hook attachment. These attachments have different uses in preparing recipes and some recipes will require specific attachments.

BASIC ATTACHMENTS

Flat Edge Beater

This attachment is an all-purpose tool, but mainly for baking recipes and mixing ingredients in general. This attachment can be employed on all speeds and used for mixing light or heavy mixtures.

Use this attachment in mixing normal to heavy mixtures:

- Cakes
- Biscuits
- Quick Breads
- Candies
- Meat Loaf
- Cookies
- Mashed Potatoes
- Pie Pastry

Wire Whip

This attachment is used to increase the volume of various mixtures by incorporating air in it like whipped cream frosting recipes, and light icing mixtures like meringue, emulsified ingredients like mayonnaise and even for your omelet recipes. It is recommended to use this attachment for faster speeds.

Use wire whip attachment for these types of recipes:

- Heavy Cream
- Mayonnaise
- Boiled Frostings
- Whipping Eggs
- Sponge Cakes
- Angel Food Cakes
- Some Candies

Dough Hook

This attachment is specifically for kneading dough mixtures for breads, especially for yeast dough. It reduces the amount of kneading time and is more convenient and faster than traditional kneading by hand. The result is almost similar and rising limitations is just about the same. It is recommended to use SPEED 2 for the attachment.

Mixtures for dough hook mixing and kneading:

- Breads
- Coffee Cakes
- Rolls
- Buns

SPECIAL ATTACHMENTS:

Aside from the basic stand mixer attachments, there are also special accessories and attachments that can be purchased for many stand mixers. These attachments aid in making daily meal prep much easier and faster. Some of these attachments make home prep of your own ingredients something that is simple and attainable. A few examples are flour, pastas, ground meat patties and sausages, pureed fruits and vegetables, homemade ice cream and many more.

Pasta Roller

This attachment is essential when you love eating homemade pastas. Freshly made pastas add a distinct taste and flavor to your favorite pasta dishes. Recommended speed for this attachment is SPEED 8 to 10.

Pasta Extruder

This attachment is used after passing the pasta dough into the rollers. The stand mixer is then attached with a mold of different shapes for making spaghetti pasta, macaroni, fusilli, fettuccine, angel hair and rigatoni. Recommended speed is SPEED 10.

Ravioli Maker

With this attachment, you can simply make homemade ravioli and cook them right away in your own kitchen. It also allows using the desired filling to be added in your freshly made ravioli. The pasta dough must be dusted first with flour and flattened in the pasta roller before using the ravioli attachment.

Food Grinder

This attachment allows grinding various ingredients such as meats, fruits, vegetables, cheese and nuts. It has a fine and coarse setting to give you the right size and texture of ground ingredients. Grinding your own ingredients and using them right away in cooking dishes will give distinct aroma and added flavor, better than store-bought ground ingredients. Use this attachment in making homemade burger patties, sausage, meatballs and the others. It is recommended to use SPEED 4 in using this attachment.

Sausage Stuffer

This attachment is used with the food grinder housing for making trouble-free homemade sausage recipes. By making your own sausage, you can ensure that the ingredients are fresh and healthy. You can also make different lengths and thickness according to preference and can be prepared ahead for future consumption. It is recommended to use SPEED 4 while using this attachment.

Vegetable Strainer

This attachment purees fresh ingredients such as tomatoes for your homemade sauce and fruits for desserts and pie fillings. Making fresh purees retains most of the nutrients and flavor making your prepared dishes more healthy and flavorful. You can also use this in straining mixtures to separate the solids like skin and the seeds. It is recommended to use SPEED 4 for this attachment.

Slicer And Shredder

With this attachment, you can now prep fruits and vegetables with uniform size and thickness. Thinly slicing potatoes, vegetables and cheese is made easier and faster by using this attachment. It can also be used in grating cheeses and fresh produce. With this attachment, you can now prepare various salads such as chopped salad or even coleslaw. SPEED 4 is recommended for this attachment.

Citrus Juicer

Refreshing beverages, luscious desserts and tasty pastries are prepared with the freshest ingredients that are available. This attachment can help you in squeezing out the juices of citrus fruits easily, while separating out the seeds from small limes to large pomegranates. Freshly squeezed juice from various citrus fruits is an essential ingredient in preparing flavorful recipes like key lime pies, citrus beverages and other desserts. It is recommended to use SPEED 6 for this attachment.

Grain Mill

With this attachment, you can now make DIY flour and cornmeal in your own kitchen. You can have finely or coarsely milled grains depending on the type of ingredient required. By using freshly milled flours, baked breads and pastries become more flavorful and nutritious because most of the grain flavor and nutrients are retained. Not like store bought flour which contains low amounts of nutrients and also with less flavor due to long periods of storage.

Ice Cream Maker

With this attachment, homemade frozen desserts and ice creams can now be prepared quickly and easily without worrying about the texture and consistency of the final product. The constant speed of the stand mixer together with controlled time durations can produce creamy, smooth, light or dense ice creams mixtures. It is recommended to place the freezer bowl inside the freezer 15 hours before making the ice cream. This allows even creaming and thickening of ice cream mixtures. Use STIR SPEED for this attachment.

Note: For more info on making ice cream with your stand mixer, be sure to check out my friend Lily Charles' book, **My Stand Mixer Ice Cream Maker Attachment Cookbook:** ***100 Deliciously Simple Homemade Recipes Using Your 2 Quart Stand Mixer Attachment for Frozen Fun.*** I highly recommend it!

Flat Beater Recipes

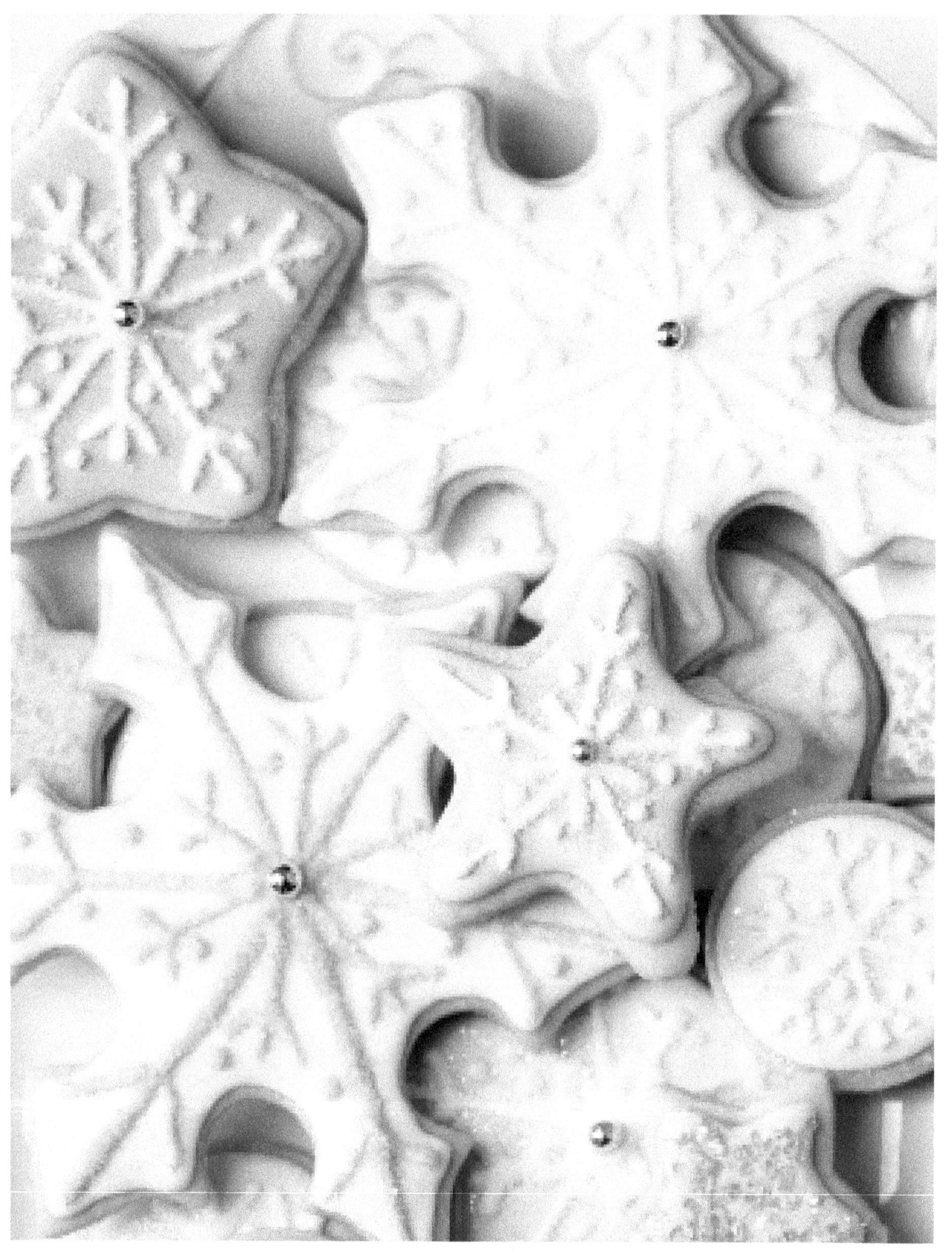

SUGAR COOKIES

I think many people have happy memories of making and decorating sugar cookies at Christmas. This is great recipe to use for cookie cutters to get those adorable shapes such as bells, stars and reindeer. I like to separate the dough into two sections and place one in the fridge while rolling and cutting the other section. This makes the dough more manageable.

Ingredients:

- 1 ½ cups softened butter
- 2 teaspoons of vanilla extract
- 4 large whole eggs, beaten
- 5 cups of sifted all-purpose flour
- 2 teaspoons of baking powder
- 1 teaspoon of salt
- 3 cups of granulated sugar

Preparation Time: 25 Minutes
Cooking Time: 6 To 8 Minutes
Yields: 24 Cookies

Directions:

1. Place the butter and sugar in the stand mixer bowl. Tilt motor head back and place the bowl securely on clamping plate. Insert flat beater onto the shaft, make sure that it is hooked properly and place lever on locking position to lock down the motor head completely.
2. Turn to "SPEED 6" and cream until the mixture is thick and smooth, or for about 1 to 2 minutes.
3. Turn to "SPEED 4", gradually add in the eggs and vanilla extract while beating constantly for about 1 to 2 minutes, or until well combined.
4. Turn off the stand mixer and scrape down the sides of the bowl with spatula. Turn to "STIR SPEED" and gradually stir in flour, salt and baking powder while mixing continuously until well incorporated. Increase mixer speed and allow mix until well blended and a dough has formed.
5. Turn off stand mixer, place lever on unlock position and lift the motor head before removing attachments.
6. Cover and place in the refrigerator to chill for at least one hour. Before baking, preheat oven to 400 degrees.
7. Use a rolling pin to flatten dough to ¼ inch thick. Use cookie cutters to cut into desired shapes and place on a baking sheet 1 inch apart. Or drop a tablespoon of cookie dough onto a baking sheet, one at a time with 2-inch spaces.
8. Place in the preheated oven and bake for about 6 to 8 minutes at 350°F, until the edges are slightly golden.
9. Remove the baking sheets from the oven and cool completely before serving or decorating.

PEANUT BUTTER COOKIES

Peanut butter cookies are one of my all-time favorite cookies and can be so versatile. Make them with the classic crisscross pattern, as the recipe suggests. Roll the dough balls in white sugar before baking and as soon as they are out of the oven press a chocolate kiss into the middle. Or perhaps one of my favorites, mix in chocolate chips and drop by rounded tablespoon onto the baking sheet creating peanut butter chocolate chip cookies. Yum, yum, yum!!!

Ingredients:

Preparation Time: 15 Minutes
Cooking Time: 10-12 Minutes
Yields: 24 Cookies

- ½ cup of light brown sugar
- ½ cup of white sugar
- 1 ¼ cups of sifted plain flour
- 1 large pinch of salt
- ½ teaspoon baking powder
- ½ teaspoon baking soda
- ¼ cup softened butter
- ½ cup unsweetened peanut butter
- 1 large whole egg
- ½ teaspoon pure vanilla extract
- Extra white sugar, for sprinkling
- ¼ cup vegetable shortening

Directions:

1. Mix together all dry ingredients in a mixing bowl, except for the sugar. Whisk gently and set aside.
2. Tilt the motor head of the stand mixer back and place the bowl securely on the clamping plate.
3. Place the butter, vegetable shortening and vanilla extract into the bowl. Attach flat beater on shaft, make sure that it is hooked properly and place lever on locking position to lock down the motor head securely.
4. Set to "SPEED 4" and cream ingredients until the mixture is thick and smooth, or for about 1 to 2 minutes. Mix in peanut butter and cream briefly just to combine.
5. Switch to "SPEED 6". Gradually add in the white and brown sugar while beating constantly for about 1 to 2 minutes, or until evenly combined. Mix in the egg and beat the mixture until well combined, or for about 1 minute.
6. Turn off the stand mixer and scrape down the sides of the bowl with spatula. Turn to "STIR SPEED" and gradually mix in flour mixture while mixing continuously until the mixture comes together.
7. Turn off stand mixer, place lever on unlock position and tilt the motor head before removing attachments. Cover dough with plastic wrap and refrigerate for several hours.
8. Rub hands with oil, take 1 tablespoon of cookie mixture and form into a ball. Repeat procedure with the remaining mixture and transfer onto the prepared baking sheet with 2-inch spaces. Lightly press down twice with a fork, forming a crisscross pattern on top of each cookie. Bake in the oven for about 10 to 12 minutes at 350°F.
9. Remove from the oven and sprinkle with white sugar on top. Let it rest to cool completely before serving or storing.

EASY TRIPLE LAYER STRAWBERRY CAKE

This is an easy way to make a delectable strawberry cake, without all the fuss dealing with strawberry puree, Which can be temperamental when baking with that much liquid. This cake uses Jello to add flavor and color without extra moisture. But don't worry, this cake is plenty moist! I recommend frosting with vanilla buttercream or cream cheese frosting.

Ingredients:

- 1 box white cake mix
- 1 (3 oz) box strawberry jello
- 2 cups of softened butter
- ½ cup whole milk
- ½ cup strawberries, finely chopped
- ½ cup sugar
- 4 large whole eggs
- ¼ all-purpose flour
- 1 cup vegetable oil

Preparation Time: 10 minutes
Cooking Time: 23 minutes
Yields: One 9-inch triple layer cake

Directions:

1. Preheat oven to 350°F and lightly grease three 9-inch baking pans. Set aside.
2. Combine together all ingredients in the mixer bowl. Tilt motor head back and place the bowl securely on clamping plate. Insert flat beater onto the shaft, make sure that it is hooked properly and place lever on locking position to lock down the motor head completely.
3. Turn mixer to "SPEED 2" and mix until ingredients are just combined. Turn off the mixer and scrape down the sides of the bowl. Increase mixer to "SPEED 4" and beat for about 3 minutes.
4. Turn off stand mixer, place lever on unlock position and lift the motor head before removing attachments. Scrape the sides of the bowl and remove from the mixer.
5. Pour the batter into the prepared baking pans and bake it in the oven for about 23 minutes. It is done when a toothpick inserted in the thickest part comes out clean.
6. Remove from the oven, transfer to a wire rack and let it rest for about 10 minutes before removing from the pans. Cool completely before frosting.

OATMEAL COOKIES

These are soft, melt-in-your-mouth cookies that taste just like they came from a bakery. Everyone will want to know your secret! The secret is to let the dough chill for a bit before baking. This gives the oats time to absorb some of the moisture and flavor in the cookie. Make them just as the recipe calls for or add raisins, dried cranberries or cherries for sweetness.

Ingredients:

Preparation Time: 15 minutes
Cooking Time: 8-10 minutes
Yields: 24 cookies

- 1 cup white sugar
- 1 cup packed brown sugar
- 2 cups sifted plain flour
- 1 teaspoon baking soda
- 1 teaspoon of salt
- 1 ½ teaspoons of cinnamon powder
- 3 cups of instant oats or rolled oats
- 1 cup of softened butter
- 2 large whole eggs
- 1 teaspoon of pure vanilla extract

Directions:

1. Preheat your oven to 375°F and lightly grease two cookie sheets or trays.
2. Mix together the flour, salt, baking soda, and cinnamon in a mixing bowl and set aside. Place the butter and brown and white sugars in the stand mixer bowl.
3. Tilt motor head back and place the bowl securely on clamping plate. Insert flat beater onto the shaft, make sure that it is hooked properly and place lever on locking position to lock down the motor head completely.
4. Turn to "SPEED 6" and cream for about 1 to 2 minutes, or until the mixture is thick and smooth.
5. Turn to "SPEED 4", gradually add in vanilla extract while beating constantly. Mix in the eggs and beat the mixture until the ingredients are evenly distributed, or for about 1 minute.
6. Turn off the stand mixer and scrape down the sides of the bowl with spatula. Turn to "STIR SPEED" and gradually stir in flour mixture while mixing continuously until well incorporated. Mix in the oats and beat further until the mixture comes together.
7. Turn off stand mixer, place lever on unlock position and lift the motor head before removing attachments. Cover bowl with plastic wrap and chill for at least an hour before baking.
8. Take about 2 tablespoons of cookie mixture, roll out to form a ball and transfer into the prepared baking sheets. Repeat the procedure with remaining mixture and lightly flatten with a fork dipped in white sugar.
9. Bake it in the oven for 8 to 10 minutes at 375°F. Remove from the oven, and let cookies rest to cool completely before serving.

CHOCOLATE CHIP COOKIES

Chocolate chip cookies are the perfect cookie. Slightly crunchy on the outside with soft chewy centers and loads of chocolate chips make this a dessert that no one in my family can turn down. I always have to double this recipe. If you prefer your cookies warm out of the oven every time, this dough freezes well. Then just pop a few on a baking tray and you'll have homemade cookies in no time. I always keep this dough on hand for when a cookie craving strikes!

Preparation Time: 15 minutes
Cooking Time: 10 minutes
Yields: 24 cookies

Ingredients:

- 1 ½ cups of all-purpose flour
- 1 teaspoon baking soda
- ½ teaspoon of salt
- ½ cup tightly packed brown sugar
- 6 tablespoons white sugar
- ½ cup unsalted butter- room temperature
- 1 large whole egg
- 1 teaspoon of pure vanilla extract
- 2 ¼ cups semi-sweet chocolate chips

Directions:

1. Preheat your oven to 350°F and lightly grease two cookie sheets or trays.
2. Mix together the flour, salt and baking soda in a mixing bowl and set aside. Place the butter and vanilla in the mixer bowl and set aside.
3. Tilt motor head back and place the bowl securely on clamping plate. Insert flat beater onto the shaft, make sure that it is hooked properly and place lever on locking position to lock down the motor head completely.
4. Turn to "SPEED 6" and cream for about 1 to 2 minutes, or until the mixture is thick and smooth.
5. Turn to "SPEED 4", gradually add in the brown and white sugar while beating constantly for about 1 to 2 minutes, or until well combined. Mix in the egg and beat the mixture until the ingredients are evenly distributed, or for about 1 minute.
6. Turn off the stand mixer and scrape down the sides of the bowl with spatula. Turn to "STIR SPEED" and gradually stir in flour mixture while mixing continuously until just incorporated. Do not over mix. Add chocolate chips, again mixing until the chips are distributed throughout the dough, but not over mixing.
7. Turn off stand mixer, place lever on unlock position and lift the motor head before removing attachments. Cover bowl with plastic wrap and chill for at least an hour before baking.
8. Take a heaping tablespoon of cookie mixture and drop it onto the prepared baking sheets. Repeat the procedure with remaining dough.
9. Bake it in the oven for about 10 minutes or until edges begin to turn a golden color. Remove from the oven and let rest to cool completely before serving.

LEMON CRINKLE COOKIES

These cookies are light, fluffy and delightfully pretty. Plus, they are lemony enough for any lemon lover out there. It does take a minute to roll each dough ball in the white sugar and the powdered sugar, but that's what gives the cookies their pretty appearance and yummy taste.

Preparation Time: 10 minutes
Cooking Time: 14-16 minutes
Yields: 24 cookies

Ingredients:

- 1 ½ cups all-purpose flour
- ¼ teaspoon baking powder
- ¼ teaspoon of salt
- 1/8 teaspoon baking soda
- ½ cup butter, softened
- 1 cup white sugar
- ½ teaspoon vanilla extract
- 1 large egg
- 1 ½ teaspoons freshly grated lemon zest
- 1 tablespoon fresh lemon juice
- ¼ cup white sugar
- ¼ cup powdered sugar
- yellow food coloring (optional)

Directions:

1. Preheat the oven to 325°F and lightly grease two cookie sheets or trays.
2. Mix together the flour, salt, baking soda, and baking powder in a mixing bowl and set aside. Place the butter and 1 cup white sugar in the mixer bowl.
3. Tilt motor head back and place the bowl securely on clamping plate. Insert flat beater onto the shaft, make sure that it is hooked properly and place lever on locking position to lock down the motor head completely.
4. Turn to "SPEED 6" and cream butter and sugar for about 1 to 2 minutes, or until the mixture is smooth and fluffy. Turn mixer to "STIR SPEED" and add the egg, vanilla extract, lemon zest and juice. If you like, add a few drops of yellow food coloring until dough reaches desired color. Gradually increase mixer speed, until ingredients are well combined.
5. Turn off the mixer and scrape down the bowl. Take small scoops, about ½ to 1 tablespoon each and roll into a ball. Roll each ball in the ¼ cup of white sugar and then in the powdered sugar. Place the cookie balls on a baking sheet, evenly spaced.
6. Bake for 14-16 minutes. When finished baking, let them cool completely.

VANILLA ALMOND BISCOTTI

This is the perfect biscotti for dunking into your coffee on a cold, winter morning. This also makes the perfect gift for neighbors and friends during the holidays. The vanilla almond flavoring is subtle and not overpowering, so it's also an excellent complement to flavored teas or coffees.

Preparation Time: 20 minutes
Cooking Time: 40-45 minutes
Yields: 30 biscotti

Ingredients:

- 1 stick unsalted butter
- 1 ¼ cups sugar
- ¼ cup light brown sugar
- 2 eggs
- 1 ½ teaspoons vanilla
- 3 cups all-purpose flour
- 1 ½ teaspoons baking powder
- ½ teaspoon salt
- ½ cup sliced almonds

Directions:

1. Add the butter and white and brown sugars to the mixing bowl.
2. Tilt motor head back and place the bowl securely on clamping plate. Insert flat beater onto the shaft, make sure that it is hooked properly and place lever on locking position to lock down the motor head completely.
3. Cream the butter and sugar using "SPEED 6" until well blended. Drop the mixer to "SPEED 4" and add the eggs, one at a time. Add vanilla and blend until well mixed.
4. In a separate bowl, stir together the remaining ingredients. Using your mixer in "STIR SPEED," add these dry ingredients into the bowl with the wet ingredients. Blend at low speed until just combined.
5. Remove the dough from the mixer and divide into two equal sections. Place each section onto a baking sheet lined with parchment paper and shape into long log about 1 inch tall and about 5 inches wide. It is best to chill the dough for about an hour before baking.
6. Preheat oven to 350°F. Bake for 30-35 minutes before removing from the oven and setting on a rack to cool. When cooled slightly, remove the logs from the baking sheet and use a knife to cut into biscotti pieces.
7. Lay the slices back on the baking sheet and bake for another 10 minutes. Remove from oven and cool slightly before removing from the baking sheet and transferring to wire rack to cool completely before storing.

BASIC SCONES

Scones are a British staple for afternoon tea or even morning coffee and they are ridiculously easy (and delicious!) You can change up the flavor by adding in a big handful of your favorite dried fruit, such a cranberries or dates.

Ingredients:

- 3 cups of sifted all-purpose flour
- ¾ cup butter, cubed
- 1 cup of whole milk
- 1 egg, beaten
- 5 teaspoons baking powder
- cup white sugar
- ½ teaspoon salt

Preparation Time: 15 minutes
Cooking Time: 15 minutes
Yields: 10 to 12 Scones

Directions:

1. Preheat the oven to 400°F and lightly grease a baking sheet. Place the flour, sugar, baking powder and salt in the mixer bowl.
2. Tilt the motor head back and place the bowl securely on the clamping plate. Attach flat beater on shaft, make sure that it is hooked properly and place lever on locking position to lock down the motor head securely.
3. Turn to "SPEED 2" and begin to add cubes of butter until the dough becomes crumbly.
4. In a separate bowl, whisk together the eggs and milk. Turn the mixer to "SPEED 4" and add the milk mixture to the dough a little at a time.
5. Turn off stand mixer, place lever on unlock position and lift the motor head before removing attachments.
6. Transfer the dough in a floured work surface and roll out into a flat round. Cut out individual rounds with a round cookie cutter. Transfer into the prepared baking tray with 2-inch space.
7. Bake it in the oven for about 15 minutes, or until lightly golden and well risen. Transfer to a wire rack, let it rest to cool completely and serve with preferred fruit preserve or cream.

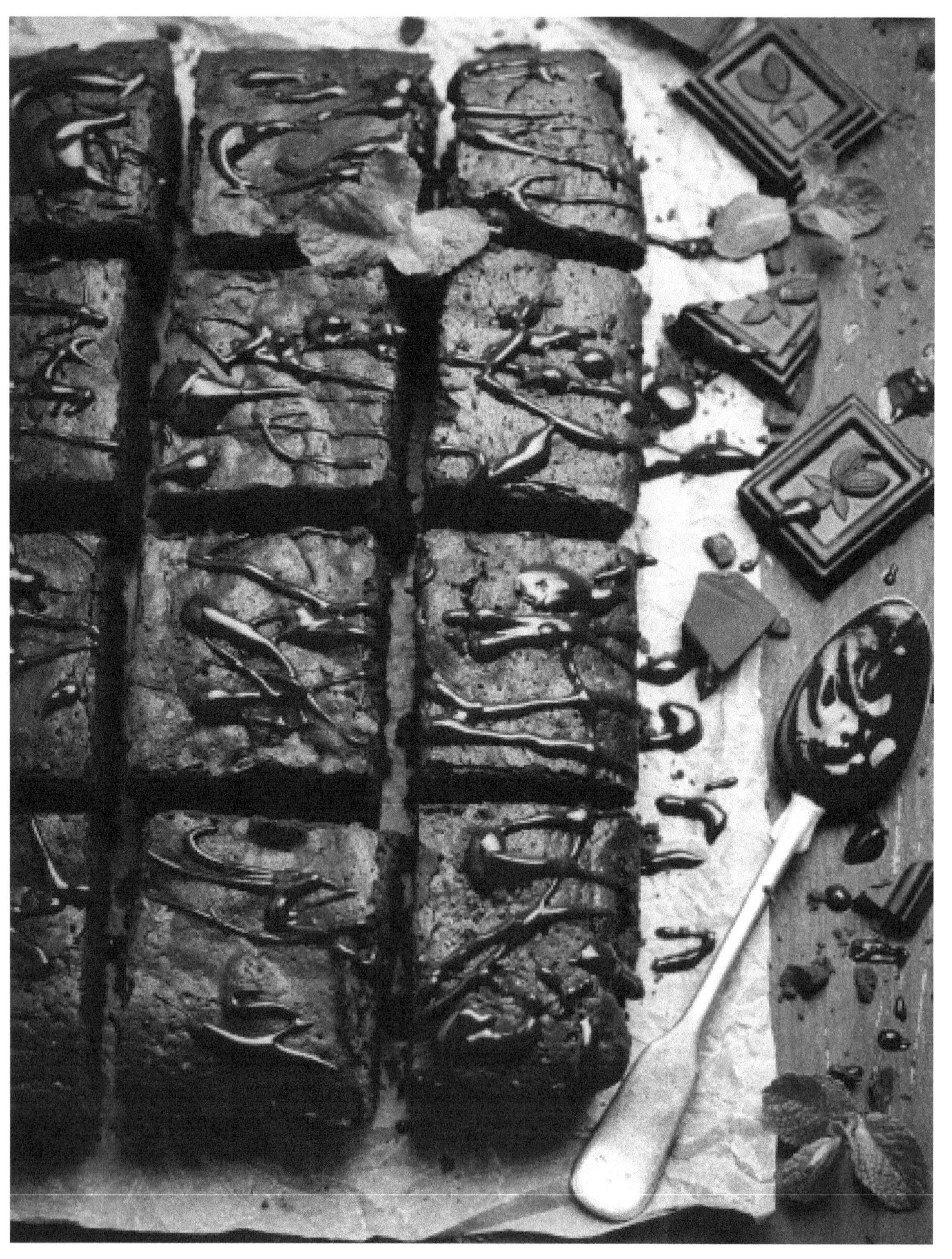

FUDGY BROWNIES

Brownies are the ultimate dessert in my house and for me…the truest way to express love. These brownies are rich and decadent and perhaps a little sinful, but who cares? These brownies stand tall like a cake brownie, but have a soft, fudgy middle and slightly crisp outer edges, making it the perfect brownie to indulge.

Ingredients:

Preparation Time: 15 minutes
Cooking Time: 35-40 minutes
Yields: 13x9 pan

- 8, 1-ounce squares of unsweetened chocolate
- 1 cup butter
- 5 eggs
- 3 cups sugar
- 1 tablespoon vanilla
- 1-1/2 cups flour
- 1 teaspoon salt
- 1 cup chocolate chips

Directions:

1. Lightly grease a 9x13 inch baking pan. Preheat your oven to 350°F.
2. Using a sauce pan set over very low heat, melt the butter and the unsweetened chocolate squares stirring frequently. Set chocolate aside when it has melted.
3. Tilt the motor head back and place the mixing bowl securely on the clamping plate. Attach flat beater on shaft, make sure that it is hooked properly and place lever on locking position to lock down the motor head securely.
4. Add to the mixing bowl the eggs, sugar and vanilla. Turn the mixer to "SPEED 8" and allow to mix for about 5 minutes.
5. Add the melted chocolate mixture and reduce to "SPEED 6." Dump in the flour and salt, continuing to mix until ingredients are just combined.
6. Gently mix in the chocolate chips and fold the batter into the greased baking dish. Bake for 35-40 minutes. Remove from the oven and allow to cool before slicing into squares.

PERFECT WHITE CAKE

White cake is like the little black dress of the baking world. You can dress it up with fancy fillings and frost it with sumptuous frostings. It's also just as good decorated in a simple vanilla buttercream or chocolate ganache. White cake is classic and never goes out of style.

Ingredients:

- 3 cups of all-purpose flour
- 2 teaspoons of baking powder
- ¼ teaspoon of salt
- 2 sticks of softened butter (1cup)
- ½ cup whole milk, room temperature
- ½ cup buttermilk, room temperature
- 2 teaspoons of vanilla extract
- ½ cup vegetable shortening
- 3 cups white sugar
- 5 eggs, room temperature

Preparation Time: 15 minutes
Cooking Time: 25-30 minutes
Yields: One triple layer 9-inch cake

Directions:

1. Preheat your oven to 350°F and lightly grease three 9-inch round cake pans. Set aside.
2. Place butter and shortening in the mixer bowl. Tilt motor head back and place the bowl securely on clamping plate. Insert flat beater onto the shaft, make sure that it is hooked properly and place lever on locking position to lock down the motor head completely. Use "SPEED 6" to cream together until light and fluffy, about 3-5 minutes.
3. Reduce to "SPEED 4" and add sugar, 1 cup at a time. Be sure to fully blend each cup before adding the next. Add eggs, one at a time, until each is well mixed.
4. In a separate mixing bowl, whisk together the flour, baking powder and salt until well combined. Mix together the milk, buttermilk and vanilla, in a separate bowl.
5. Turn stand mixer to "STIR SPEED", gradually add half of the flour mixture. When mostly blended, add in the milk mixture and finally add the last of the flour mixture. Beat until the ingredients are just evenly distributed. Scrape down the sides of the bowl, turn to "SPEED 6" and beat until smooth and well incorporated.
6. Turn off stand mixer, place lever on unlock position and lift the motor head before removing attachments. Scrape the sides of the bowl and remove from the mixer.
7. Divide and pour the batter into the prepared pans and bake it in the oven for about 25-30 minutes. It is done when a toothpick inserted on the thickest part comes out clean.
8. Remove from the oven, transfer to a wire rack and cool for about 10 minutes. Invert the pans to remove the cakes and let cool completely before frosting.

MAPLE FUDGE CANDIES

This is a simple, delicious candy that literally melts in your mouth. If you don't have a good candy thermometer, it's a good investment and they aren't expensive. Store the cut candies up to a week in an air-tight container so they don't get crumbly. I'll bet they won't last that long!

Ingredients:

- Oil, for greasing
- ¼ teaspoon of baking soda
- 2 cups packed light brown sugar
- 1 cup of heavy whipping cream
- ¼ cup cubed butter
- ½ cup of pure maple syrup
- ½ teaspoon pure vanilla extract

Preparation Time: 2 hours
Cooking Time: 5-10 minutes
Yields: 24 candy pieces

Directions:

1. Line a square 8x8 baking dish with parchment paper and lightly grease the mixer bowl. Set aside.
2. Mix together the maple syrup, sugar, baking soda, butter and cream in a saucepan and apply medium heat. Cook until a candy thermometer registers 240°F while stirring constantly and immediately transfer into the greased mixing bowl. Let it rest to cool for about 1 ½ to 2 hours.
3. Add in the vanilla extract, tilt motor head back and place the bowl securely on clamping plate. Insert flat beater onto the shaft, make sure that it is hooked properly and place lever on locking position to lock down the motor head completely.
4. Turn to "STIR SPEED" and beat for about 6 to 8 minutes.
5. Turn off stand mixer, place lever on unlock position and lift the motor head. Transfer candy mixture into the prepared baking dish and scrape to remove candy mixture on the sides.
6. Let it cool completely, flip onto a cutting board and cut into squares.

CHOCOLATE CAKE WITH CHOCOLATE CREAM CHEESE FROSTING p. 32

CHOCOLATE CAKE WITH CHOCOLATE CREAM CHEESE FROSTING

When we were first dating, my husband professed his hatred of all things cream cheese. So, I used to sneak it into recipes…a cream sauce here, cream cheese frosting there. He would go on and on about how much he loved what he was eating and later I would tell him that one of the main ingredients was cream cheese. While he still won't eat a cream cheese bagel, he will now openly admit to loving this chocolate cream cheese frosted cake and requests it for most birthdays.

Preparation Time: 15 minutes
Cooking Time: 30-35 minutes
Yields: One triple layer 9 inch cake

Ingredients:

For the Cake:

- 3 cups of all-purpose flour
- 3 cups white sugar
- 1 ½ cups unsweetened cocoa powder
- 1 tablespoon baking soda
- 1 ½ teaspoons salt
- 1 ½ teaspoons baking powder
- 1 ½ cups buttermilk
- 4 large eggs
- ½ cup vegetable oil
- 2 teaspoons vanilla extract
- 1 ½ cups warm water
- Butter and flour, for greasing

For the Frosting:

- 1 ½ cups butter, softened
- 8 ounces cream cheese, softened
- 1 cup unsweetened cocoa powder
- ½ cup dark unsweetened cocoa powder
- 3 teaspoons vanilla extract
- 7-8 cups powdered sugar
- ¼ cup milk, as needed

Directions:

1. Preheat your oven to 350°F and lightly grease three, round 9-inch cake pans with butter and then dust with flour.
2. Tilt the stand mixer motor head back and place the bowl securely on clamping plate of stand mixer. Insert flat beater onto the shaft, make sure that it is hooked properly and place lever on locking position to lock down the motor head completely.
3. On a low speed, mix together flour, cocoa powder, sugar, salt, baking soda and baking powder.
4. Add the eggs, oil, warm water, buttermilk and vanilla in the mixer bowl, set to "SPEED 6" and cream until smooth and fluffy. Beat until the ingredients are evenly distributed.
5. Turn off stand mixer, place lever on unlock position and lift the motor head before removing attachments. Scrape down the sides, divide into 3 equal portions and transfer into the prepared cake pans.
6. Bake it in the oven for 30 to 35 minutes, or until a toothpick inserted on the thickest part comes out clean. Remove from the oven, transfer to a wire rack and let it rest to cool.
7. Invert onto a cutting board to remove cake from pans and allow to cool completely.
8. To make frosting: Start with a clean bowl and beater. Add butter and cream cheese to the mixing bowl and set to "SPEED 6." Beat until fluffy.
9. Set to "SPEED 4", gradually mix in the cocoa powder and vanilla. Beat until smooth and well incorporated.
10. Add in 1 cup of powdered sugar at a time. If it becomes too thick, add milk, 1 tablespoon at a time to make frosting more spreadable. The frosting is meant to be thick.
11. Turn off stand mixer, unlock and tilt back the motor head. Scrape down the sides and remove the bowl from the stand mixer.
12. Place one layer of cake on a rotating cake stand, cover the top with frosting and spread evenly with a spatula. Repeat the procedure with the remaining layers of cake and spread a thin frosting on the last layer.
13. Chill for at least 15 minutes or until set and cover the cake completely with the remaining frosting and smooth out evenly with a spatula.
14. Chill for another 15 minutes before slicing and serving.

BASIC PIE CRUST

Sure, you could buy a pre-made pie crust from the store, but those can be troublesome to work with and do not taste anywhere near as good as this homemade one does. Flaky and buttery, this pie crust will elevate your pies to the next level, and it's really easy using your stand mixer. Impress everyone at holiday family gatherings by bringing a pie with a homemade crust!

Ingredients:

Preparation Time: 15 minutes
Yields: Two pie crusts

- ¼ cup of light brown sugar
- 2 cups of sifted plain flour
- 1 large pinch of salt
- 1 cup cubed butter
- Cold water, as needed
- Extra flour, for dusting

Directions:

1. Tilt motor head back and place the bowl securely on clamping plate. Insert flat beater onto the shaft, make sure that it is hooked properly and place lever on locking position to lock down the motor head completely.
2. Place the flour, sugar and salt in the mixer bowl. Set to "STIR SPEED" and mix until well combined. Add in the butter and beat until the mixture is crumbly.
3. Gradually add in ¼ cup of cold water while beating constantly until the mixture starts to cling on the paddle. Adjust consistency if the mixture is too dry by slowly adding more cold water just until it comes together.
4. Turn off stand mixer, place lever on unlock position and lift the motor head before removing attachments. Scrape down the sides and transfer the mixture on a floured work surface.
5. Divide the dough into 2 equal portions and roll out into 12-inch flat rounds. Cover with foil or plastic wrap and freeze for future use.

RED VELVET LAYER CAKE p. 36

RED VELVET LAYER CAKE

If prepared correctly, red velvet cake is so fluffy and moist. And it has that beautiful red coloring, making it the perfect special occasion cake. The key is not to over-mix the ingredients. Stir until everything is blended, but don't continue to mix. If you want to make this into a four layer cake, gently slice each cake in half lengthwise to wind up with 4 thin cake layers or just use them as they are for a delicious double layer cake.

Preparation Time: 15 minutes
Cooking Time: 35-40 minutes
Yields: One-four layer 9-inch cake

Ingredients:

For the Cake:

- 3 cups of sifted cake flour
- 3 tablespoons of unsweetened cocoa powder
- 1 teaspoon of baking soda
- ½ teaspoon salt
- 2 cups sifted white sugar
- 2 teaspoons of red food dye
- ¾ to 1 cup softened butter
- 1 cup of buttermilk
- ¼ cup vegetable shortening
- 3 large whole eggs, beaten
- 1 tablespoon of apple cider vinegar
- 1 teaspoon of pure vanilla extract
- Butter or oil, for greasing

For the Frosting:

- 4 cups softened cream cheese
- 2 cups softened butter
- 6 to 7 cups of confectioners' sugar
- 2 teaspoons of lemon juice
- ½ teaspoon of pure vanilla extract
- 1 small pinch of salt

Directions:

1. Preheat your oven to 350°F and lightly grease two round 9-inch cake pans with butter. Line cake pans with parchment paper and lightly brush with butter.
2. Mix together the cocoa powder, baking soda, salt, and cake flour in a mixing bowl until well combined, set aside.

3. Tilt the stand mixer motor head back and place the bowl securely on clamping plate. Insert flat beater onto the shaft, make sure that it is hooked properly and place lever on locking position to lock down the motor head completely.
4. Add the butter, shortening and sugar in the mixer bowl, set to "SPEED 6" and cream until smooth and fluffy. Add the eggs one at a time while beating constantly and mix in the vinegar, vanilla and red food dye. Beat further until the ingredients are evenly distributed.
5. Set to "SPEED 4", slowly add in half of the flour mixture and add half of the buttermilk while beating constantly until well combined. Mix in the remaining flour mixture and buttermilk while beating continuously until just incorporated.
6. Turn off stand mixer, place lever on unlock position and lift the motor head before removing attachments. Scrape down the sides, divide into 2 portions and transfer into the prepared cake pans.
7. Bake it in the oven for 35 to 40 minutes, or until a toothpick inserted on the thickest part comes out clean. Remove from the oven, transfer to a wire rack and let it rest to cool completely.
8. Invert onto a cutting board and slice with a bread knife on the middle part to have two round layers. Set aside.
9. Wipe the flat beater and mixing bowl with cloth and reattach into the stand mixer. Add the butter and cheese and beat on "SPEED 6" until smooth and fluffy.
10. Set to "SPEED 4", gradually mix in the sugar while beating constantly and stir in the rest of the ingredients. Beat until smooth and well incorporated.
11. Turn off stand mixer, unlock and tilt back the motor head. Scrape down the sides and remove the bowl from the stand mixer.
12. Place one layer of cake on a rotating cake stand, cover the top with frosting and spread evenly with a spatula. Repeat the procedure with the remaining layer of cake and spread a thin frosting on the last layer.
13. Chill for at least 15 minutes or until set and cover the cake completely with the remaining frosting and smooth out evenly with a spatula.
14. Chill for another 15 minutes before slicing and serving.

ALMOND-CHOCOLATE CHIP PIE

I like to think of this pie as part chocolate chip cookie, part pie and 100% delicious. This is an old recipe from a dear southern friend, so you know it's going to be good! For the best pie, use a homemade pie crust.

Ingredients:

- 1pre-made pie crust
- 1 cup packed brown sugar
- ¼ cup softened butter
- 1 medium whole egg
- 1 ½ teaspoons of pure vanilla extract
- ½ teaspoon baking powder
- 1 large pinch of salt
- 1 cup of sifted flour
- 1 cup of semisweet chocolate chips
- ¼ cup toasted almonds, chopped

Preparation Time: 15 minutes
Cooking Time: 25-30 minutes
Yields: 8 to 10 servings

Directions:

1. Place the pie crust in the pie plate and press down the sides and bottom part to cover the plate completely.
2. Preheat the oven to 350°F.
3. Tilt motor head back and place the bowl securely on clamping plate. Insert flat beater onto the shaft, make sure that it is hooked properly and place lever on locking position to lock down the motor head completely.
4. Mix together the flour, salt and baking powder until well combined and set aside.
5. Turn to "SPEED 6" and cream the sugar and butter until thick and smooth. Add in the egg and vanilla extract and beat until well combined.
6. Turn to "SPEED 4, gradually add the flour mixture while beating constantly until well incorporated. Mix in half the chocolate chips and beat until just combined.
7. Turn off stand mixer, place lever on unlock position and lift the motor head before removing attachments. Scrape down the sides, transfer the mixture into the prepared pie plate and spread evenly.
8. Top with the remaining chocolate and nuts and bake it in the oven for about 25 to 30 minutes. Remove from the oven, transfer to a wire rack and let it rest to cool completely before slicing.
9. Slice the pie, transfer to a serving platter and serve right away.

CARROT CAKE WITH CREAM CHEESE FROSTING p. 40

CARROT CAKE WITH CREAM CHEESE FROSTING

A staple for most Easter celebrations, but delicious anytime of year, this carrot cake recipe has raisins and walnuts for added taste and texture. If you have a stand mixer shredding attachment, use it to shred your carrots, quick and easy. If not, or if you prefer a finer shred, use a hand grater. This is a moist, yummy cake that you will be proud to serve to family and friends.

Ingredients:

Preparation Time: 45 minutes
Cooking Time: 35-40 minutes
Yields: One double layer 9-inchcake

For the Carrot Cake:

- Butter or cooking oil, for greasing
- 2 cups sifted plain flour
- ½ teaspoon of baking soda
- 1 teaspoon of baking powder
- ½ teaspoon fine salt
- 1 ½ teaspoons of cinnamon powder
- ½ teaspoon of pumpkin spice
- ½ teaspoon nutmeg powder
- 4 fresh whole eggs, beaten
- 2 cups sifted light brown sugar
- 1 cup of canola or safflower oil
- 3 cups of grated or minced carrots

Additional Ingredients:

- ¼ cup toasted and chopped pecans or walnuts
- ¼ cup seedless raisins

For the Frosting:

- 2 cups chilled cream cheese
- ¾ cup of softened butter
- 1 ¼ cups of sifted confectioners' sugar
- 2 teaspoons of vanilla extract

Directions:

1. Preheat your oven to 375°F and position a rack on the middle. Lightly grease two round 9x2 inch cake pans and line the bottom with parchment paper.
2. Add all dry ingredients for the cake in a mixing bowl, except for the sugar and mix until well combined. Set aside.
3. Tilt the stand mixer motor head back and place the bowl securely on clamping plate. Insert flat beater onto the shaft, make sure that it is hooked properly and place lever on locking position to lock down the motor head completely.
4. Place the sugar in the bowl, turn to "STIR SPEED" and add the eggs one at a time while beating continuously until smooth and well combined.
5. Turn off stand mixer, unlock motor head and remove the flat beater. Wipe the flat beater with cloth, reattach into the stand mixer and scrape down the sides of the bowl.
6. Turn to "SPEED 6" and gradually pour in the oil while beating constantly until well combined. Turn to "SPEED 4" and add the flour mixture in 3 separate batches while beating constantly until the ingredients are evenly distributed.
7. Turn to "STIR SPEED" and mix in the carrots, nuts and raisins with the mixture. Beat mixture briefly until the ingredients are evenly distributed.
8. Turn off stand mixer, place lever on unlock position and lift the motor head before removing attachments. Scrape down the sides and remove the bowl from the stand mixer.
9. Portion the mixture into the prepared cake pans and bake it in the oven for about 35 to 40 minutes. It is done when a toothpick inserted on the thickest part comes out clean.
10. Remove from the oven, let it rest for 5 minutes to cool and invert cake onto a rack. Let it rest to cool completely before slicing and remove the parchment paper. Invert onto a large plate and set aside.
11. Wipe the bowl and flat beater with cloth and reattach into the stand mixer. Place the butter and cream cheese in the mixing bowl, set to "SPEED 6" and cream until smooth and fluffy. Set to "SPEED 4" and gradually add in the sugar while beating constantly and add the vanilla. Beat further until smooth and well incorporated while scraping the sides with a spatula.
12. Turn off stand mixer, unlock and lift the motor head and remove the bowl from the mixer. Place one layer of cake on a rotating cake stand, cover the top with frosting and spread evenly with a spatula. Invert the next layer of cake on top and cover completely with the remaining frosting.
13. Sprinkle with extra chopped nuts on top if desired and slice into wedges before serving.

POUND CAKE

Did you know that original pound cakes were created using a 1:1:1:1 ratio of butter, sugar, flour and eggs? Somewhere in time, a few more ingredients have been added to many recipes for extra flavor. Bake this pound cake in a Bundt pan and sprinkle lightly with powdered sugar when it has cooled.

Ingredients:

- 3 cups of sifted plain flour
- 2 cups sifted white sugar
- 2 teaspoons of baking powder
- ½ teaspoon of salt
- 2 cups of softened butter
- ½ cup whole milk
- ½ teaspoon of pure vanilla extract
- ½ teaspoon of almond extract
- 6 large whole eggs

Preparation Time: 20 minutes
Cooking Time: 1 hour-1 hour 15 minutes
Yields: one 10-inch cake

Directions:

1. Preheat your oven to 350°F and lightly grease a 10-inch tube pan with oil or butter. Set aside.
2. Combine together all dry ingredients in the mixer bowl. Tilt motor head back and place the bowl securely on clamping plate. Insert flat beater onto the shaft, make sure that it is hooked properly and place lever on locking position to lock down the motor head completely.
3. In a separate mixing bowl, whisk together the butter and vanilla until well combined and add in the milk and almond extract. Mix until well incorporated.
4. Turn stand mixer to "STIR SPEED", gradually add liquid mixture into the flour mixture and beat until the ingredients are evenly distributed. Scrape down the sides of the bowl, turn to "SPEED 6" and beat until smooth and well incorporated.
5. Add the eggs one at a time while beating constantly on "SPEED 4" until well incorporated.
6. Turn off stand mixer, place lever on unlock position and lift the motor head before removing attachments. Scrape the sides of the bowl and remove from the mixer.
7. Pour the batter into the prepared tube pans and bake it in the oven for about 1 hour to 1 hour and 15 minutes. It is done when a toothpick inserted on the thickest part comes out clean.
8. Remove from the oven, transfer to a wire rack and let it rest completely before slicing and serving.

BLUEBERRY MUFFINS

The perfect breakfast treat, these blueberry muffins are just the right blend of sweet muffin and juicy berries. For light and fluffy muffins, use your mixer to blend in the flour until it is just incorporated, but do not over mix.

Ingredients:

Preparation Time: 15 minutes
Cooking Time: 30-35 minutes
Yields: 12 muffins

- 2 cups of flour
- 1 ¼ cups white sugar
- 2 teaspoons of baking powder
- ½ cup of softened butter
- ½ teaspoon salt
- ½ cup milk
- 1 teaspoon vanilla extract
- 2 large eggs
- 2 cups blueberries, rinsed and drained
- 3 teaspoons sugar, for sprinkling

Directions:

1. Preheat the oven to 375°F and place 12 cupcake liners into a muffin tin.
2. Add butter and white sugar into the mixer bowl. Tilt motor head back and place the bowl securely on clamping plate. Insert flat beater onto the shaft, make sure that it is hooked properly and place lever on locking position to lock down the motor head completely. Turn mixer to "SPEED 6" and cream the butter and sugar until light and fluffy.
3. Slow the mixer speed, and add the eggs, one at a time. Beat well in between each egg. Stir in the vanilla extract.
4. In a separate mixing bowl, whisk together the flour, baking powder and salt.
5. Turn stand mixer to "STIR SPEED", gradually add half of the flour mixture. Add the milk and then add the remaining flour mixture and beat until the ingredients are evenly distributed. Scrape down the sides of the bowl, turn to "SPEED 6" and beat until just blended.
6. Use a fork to smash ½ cup of the blueberries. Add these to the batter and mix to blend. Add the remaining whole blueberries and use "STIR SPEED" briefly to distribute the berries.
7. Fill the lined muffin tins each about 2/3 full with the batter. Sprinkle with remaining white sugar. Bake for 30-35 minutes, until tops are golden brown and muffins are cooked through.
8. Remove from the oven, transfer to a wire rack and let cool. When cool enough, remove muffins from the pan and either serve warm or let them cool completely before storing.

STREUSEL LAYERED COFFEE CAKE

This coffee cake is perfect for breakfast, brunch or dessert. I'm not even a big fan of coffee cake, but this one is moist and has a yummy, cinnamon sweet strudel layer. It makes a full 9x13 pan so it is plenty to feed a crowd.

Ingredients:

Preparation Time: 20 *minutes*
Cooking Time: 55 *minutes*
Yields: 9x13 *pan*

Streusel

- 2/3 cup packed brown sugar
- 1 and 1/3 cups all-purpose flour
- 3 teaspoons ground cinnamon
- ½ teaspoon salt
- 1 stick (8 tablespoons) cold butter, cubed

Cake

- 2 ½ cups all-purpose flour
- 2 teaspoons baking powder
- 1 teaspoon baking soda
- ½ teaspoon salt
- 2 teaspoons vanilla extract
- 1 ½ sticks unsalted butter, softened
- 3 eggs
- 1 ½ cups white sugar
- 1 ¼ cups sour cream or plain Greek yogurt

Directions:

1. Preheat your oven to 350°F and lightly grease a 9x13 pan with oil or butter. Set aside.
2. Combine together all streusel ingredients except the butter in the mixer bowl. Tilt motor head back and place the bowl securely on clamping plate. Insert flat beater onto the shaft, make sure that it is hooked properly and place lever on locking position to lock down the motor head completely.
3. Turn mixer to "STIR SPEED" and mix the items. Slowly add the cubes of butter, a few at a time, until the mixture becomes crumbly and all butter has been added. Remove streusel ingredients from the mixer bowl and set aside in another bowl.
4. Place the mixer bowl back on the mixer and lock into place. Cream together butter and sugar. Add the vanilla and eggs, one at a time. Finally, add sour cream. Scrape bowl to bring all ingredients to the middle.
5. Beginning with"STIR SPEED" and increasing as necessary, add the flour, baking soda, baking powder and salt to the mixture. Mix until ingredients are combined.
6. Pour half of the cake batter into your prepared pan. Top with about a third of the streusel topping. Pour remaining batter over top of the streusel layer. Finally, sprinkle on the rest of the streusel topping evenly.
7. Bake for about 55 minutes, until streusel topping turns golden in color.
8. Remove from the oven, transfer to a wire rack and let it cool before slicing and serving.

PUMPKIN ROLL WITH CREAM CHEESE FILLING

If you need a dessert for impressing guests, this is one to consider. Rolling the cake in a towel while still warm keeps the cake from crumbling later when the filling is added. You can also freeze this cake. Thaw mostly before serving as it slices best when just slightly frozen.

Ingredients:

Preparation Time: 25 minutes
Cooking Time: 30 to 35 minutes
Yields: 8 Servings

For the Cake:

- 3 large whole eggs
- 1 cup packed white sugar
- ¾ cup of pumpkin puree
- 1 teaspoon of baking soda
- 1 teaspoon of cinnamon powder
- ½ teaspoon nutmeg
- 1 cup sifted flour
- Icing sugar, for dusting

For the Cream Cheese Filling:

- 1 cup softened cream cheese
- ¼ cup softened butter, softened
- 1 cup of sifted confectioner's sugar
- 1 teaspoon of pure vanilla extract

Directions:

1. Preheat your oven to 350°F, lightly grease a 10x14 rimmed baking pan with butter and line with parchment paper. Grease and lightly flour the parchment.
2. Place the sugar, pumpkin and eggs in the mixer bowl. In a separate bowl, whisk together the remaining ingredients and set aside.
3. Tilt motor head back and place the bowl with eggs, sugar and pumpkin securely on clamping plate. Insert flat beater onto the shaft, make sure that it is hooked properly and place lever on locking position to lock down the motor head completely.
4. Set to "SPEED 4", beat until well combined and gradually add in the flour. Beat mixture until well incorporated.

5. Turn off stand mixer, place lever on unlock position and lift the motor head before removing attachments. Scrape down the sides and remove the bowl from the stand mixer.
6. Add the pumpkin mixture to the baking pan and spread evenly with a spatula. Bake it in the oven for about 30 to 35 minutes, or until a toothpick inserted on the thickest part comes out clean.
7. While baking the roll, prepare the cream cheese filling. Clean the flat beater and bowl and reattach to the mixer.
8. Add all ingredients into the bowl, set to "SPEED 4" and beat until smooth and well incorporated. Turn off stand mixer, remove bowl and set aside.
9. When the pumpkin roll is done, remove it from the oven.
10. Remove from the pan, remove the parchment paper and trim off any brown sides. Place the cake on a clean towel and roll up. Allow to cool while wrapped with the towel.
11. When cool, unroll the cake from the towel and top with the filling. Spread evenly with a spatula.
12. Hold two corners on the bottom of the cake and slowly roll upwards.Roll the cake up again with the filling now in the center. Lightly wrap in wax paper and place in the refrigerator to chill before serving.

PEAR, APPLE AND CRANBERRY CRISP

The perfect fall treat, this recipe is easy and tasty. Although it doesn't utilize the stand mixer a lot, I like to have the stand mixer make the toppings when working with cut butter. This way seems to more evenly distribute the ingredients and it's no hassle stirring for me.

Ingredients:

Preparation Time: 20 minutes
Cooking Time: 1 hour
Yields: 9x13 pan

For the Filling:

- 4 large pears, cored and peeled, diced
- 4 large red apples, cored and peeled, diced
- 1 small orange, zested and juiced
- 1 large lemon, zested and juiced
- ½ cup dried cranberries
- ½ cup of white sugar
- ¼ cup sifted plain flour
- 1 teaspoon of cinnamon powder
- ½ teaspoon nutmeg powder

For the topping:

- 1 ½ cups sifted plain flour
- ¾ cup sifted white sugar
- ½ cup sifted raw cane sugar, lightly packed
- ½ teaspoon fine sea salt
- 1 cup steel-cut oats, 1 cup cubed, chilled butter

Directions:

1. Preheat your oven to 350°F. Lightly grease a 9x13 baking dish.
2. Mix together all dry ingredients for the filling in a large mixing bowl and mix until well combined. Add in the remaining ingredients and toss to evenly coat the fruits with the flour mixture. Transfer into a baking dish and set aside.
3. Add all ingredients for the topping in the mixer bowl, set aside.
4. Tilt motor head back and place the bowl securely on clamping plate. Insert flat beater onto the shaft, make sure that it is hooked properly and place lever on locking position to lock down the motor head completely.
5. Set to "STIR SPEED" and beat briefly until the mixture is crumbly. Turn off stand mixer, place lever on unlock position and lift the motor head.
6. Sprinkle the topping mixture evenly on top of the fruits and bake it in the oven for about 50 to 60 minutes, or until the fruit is bubbly and the top is golden brown. Remove from the oven, transfer to a wire rack and let it rest for 10 minutes before serving.

PEPPERMINT PATTIES

Peppermint patties are one of my favorite candies and are really so easy to make at home. When making the filling, you don't want it to be sticky. Add powdered sugar until a firm but pliable filling is formed.

Ingredients:

- 12 ounces of chocolate melting wafers
- 2 cups sifted confectioner's sugar
- ¼ cup softened butter
- ¼ cup full-fat cream
- 1 teaspoon of pure peppermint extract

Preparation Time: 30 minutes
Yields: 36 candy pieces

Directions:

1. Combine together the butter, sugar, cream and peppermint extract in the mixer bowl. Cut a 12x12 inch piece of cling wrap for the filling. Line a baking sheet with parchment paper and set aside.
2. Tilt motor head back and place the bowl securely on clamping plate. Insert flat beater onto the shaft, make sure that it is hooked properly and place lever on locking position to lock down the motor head completely.
3. Turn to "STIR SPEED and beat briefly just to combine. Turn to "SPEED 4" and beat mixture until it comes together. If the mixture is too wet, add more powdered sugar while beating constantly until the desired consistency is achieved.
4. Turn off stand mixer, place lever on unlock position and lift the motor head before removing attachments. Scrape down the sides and transfer the mixture into the prepared cling wrap. Roll the mixture to form into a 1 ½-inch tube and twist both ends to secure the mixture.
5. Chill candy mixture for at least 1 hour or until firm. Transfer to a cutting board and slice into thin rounds. Place the rounds on a baking sheet and chill before dipping.
6. Place the chocolate wafers in microwaveable bowl and melt in the microwave for about 1 to 2 minutes, while stirring every 30 seconds to prevent burning.
7. Dip the peppermint candies completely in the melted chocolate. Transfer to the parchment lined baking sheet and let it rest at room temperature until set.
8. Serve when chocolate has hardened or store in an airtight container in the refrigerator.

SWEET POTATO PIE

Whether you are making it for Thanksgiving or just to spruce up an ordinary day, this pie is sure to be loved by all. Our family likes to pretend that sweet potato pie is healthy, but really with that much butter and sugar, it's much more of a treat!

Ingredients:

Preparation Time: 20 minutes
Cooking Time: 40- 50 minutes
Yields: 8 to 10 slices

- 1 pre-made pie crust
- 1 pound of sweet potatoes, peeled and cubed
- ½ cup cubed and softened butter
- 1 ¼ cups white sugar
- 2 large whole eggs
- ½ teaspoon of allspice powder
- 1 teaspoon cinnamon powder
- ½ teaspoon nutmeg powder
- ½ to 1 teaspoon of pure vanilla extract
- 1 lemon, juiced
- Extra flour, for dusting

Directions:

1. Place the pie crust in the pie plate and press down the sides and bottom part to cover the plate completely. Cover with plastic wrap and chill before use.
2. Pour 2 cups of water into a saucepan, apply medium-high heat and bring to a boil. Fit a steamer basket into the saucepan, place the potatoes and steam for 1 hour or until tender. Let it rest for about 10 minutes to cool.
3. Preheat your oven to 375°F.
4. Tilt motor head back and place the bowl securely on clamping plate. Insert flat beater onto the shaft, make sure that it is hooked properly and place lever on locking position to lock down the motor head completely.
5. Place the potatoes in the kitchen mixer bowl, turn to "STIR SPEED" and beat until evenly mashed.
6. Add the butter, turn to "STIR SPEED" and beat until the butter is evenly distributed.
7. Gradually add in the sugar while beating constantly, add in one egg at a time and beat further and until well combined. Stir in the rest of the ingredients and beat until well incorporated.
8. Turn off stand mixer, place lever on unlock position and lift the motor head before removing attachments. Scrape down the sides and transfer the mixture into the prepared pie plate. Spread evenly with a spatula and bake it in the oven for about 40 to 50 minutes, or until the center is set and cooked thoroughly.
9. Remove from the oven, transfer to a wire rack and let it rest for 10 to 15 minutes before slicing. Slice into 8 to 12 wedges and serve immediately.

PASSION FRUIT MOUSSE

This unique Brazilian dessert is simple to make and so refreshing. Shop for passion fruit pulp in most groceries or specialty food stores.

Ingredients:

Preparation Time: 10 minutes
Yields: 8 servings

- 4 cups of heavy whipping cream
- 2 cups chilled passion fruit pulp in syrup
- 1 ½ cups of sweetened condensed milk
- Shaved ice, for serving
- Fresh mint leaves, for serving
- Biscotti, for serving

Directions:

1. In 8 serving glasses or martini glasses, add a tablespoon of passion fruit pulp syrup on the bottom and set aside. Reserve 4 tablespoons for serving.
2. Mix condensed milk and the remaining passion fruit pulp in a mixing bowl and whisk until well combined.
3. Tilt motor head back and place the bowl securely on clamping plate. Insert flat beater onto the shaft, make sure that it is hooked properly and place lever on locking position to lock down the motor head completely.
4. Pour the cream in the mixer bowl, set to "SPEED 4" and beat for 30 seconds. Gradually turn to "SPEED 6" and beat until stiff peaks form.
5. Turn off stand mixer and remove ¾ of the whipped cream and reserve. Add the passion fruit and milk mixture in the mixer bowl and beat on "STIR SPEED" until well combined. Scrape down the sides and gradually add the reserved cream while beating constantly until well incorporated. Turn off mixer, unlock and lift the motor head to remove the bowl.
6. Add 2 to 3 tablespoons of shaved ice in each serving glass and fill with passion fruit mousse, or chill mixture before serving. Top with reserved passion fruit pulp and mint and serve immediately with biscotti.

MEATLOAF

My family loves meatloaf, but I always hate mixing up the ingredients. Everything is so cold and messy, and it just doesn't mix well with a spoon. This meatloaf is perfectly mixed with your mixer and you don't have to have cold, grimy hands!

Ingredients:

Preparation Time: 15 minutes
Yields: 1 stick of butter

- 2 pounds of ground lean beef
- ½ teaspoon salt
- ½ teaspoon ground black pepper
- ½ teaspoon garlic powder
- ¾cup toasted breadcrumbs
- ½ cup diced onion
- ½cup of diced bell pepper
- ½cup ketchup
- 2 large whole eggs

For the topping:

- ½ cup of tomato sauce
- ½ teaspoon dried oregano
- ½ tablespoon minced fresh basil
- 1 tablespoon of sugar
- 1 tablespoon prepared mustard

Directions:

1. Preheat the oven to 350°F. Mix together pepper, salt, garlic powder and breadcrumbs in a small bowl and set aside.
2. Mix together all topping sauce ingredients in another mixing bowl until well combined, set aside.
3. Tilt motor head back and place the bowl securely on clamping plate. Insert flat beater onto the shaft, make sure that it is hooked properly and place lever on locking position to lock down the motor head completely.
4. Place the ground meat, ketchup, onion, pepper and eggs in the stand mixer bowl and set to "STIR SPEED". Beat until well combined and slowly add in the breadcrumb mixture.
5. Set to "SPEED 2" and beat until well incorporated.
6. Turn off stand mixer, place lever on unlock position and lift the motor head to remove the bowl.
7. Place the ground meat mixture in a baking dish and form into a loaf shape. Spread the tomato sauce topping evenly on top.
8. Bake it in the oven for 1 hour to 1 hour and 15 minutes, or until the top is lightly browned and cooked through. Remove from the oven and let it rest for about 10 minutes before serving.

SWEDISH MEATBALLS

When I first got my stand mixer, I was amazed at all the uses that I had never even considered. Using your stand mixer to prep meatballs is the perfect way to get well-blended meatballs while doing minimal work.

Preparation Time: 20 minutes
Cooking Time: 30 minutes
Yields: 4 servings

Ingredients:

For the Meatloaf:

- ½ pound ground chuck (15% fat content)
- ½ pound ground veal
- ½ cup chopped onion
- 3 tablespoons butter
- 1 piece of white bread, torn into 4 pieces
- ½ cup whole milk
- 1 large egg
- 1 ½ teaspoons salt
- ¾ teaspoon black pepper
- ½ teaspoon ground nutmeg
- 2 tablespoons all-purpose flour
- 2 cups beef broth
- ½ cup sour cream
- 3 tablespoons fresh chopped parsley

Directions:

1. In a large skillet, over medium heat, melt 1 tablespoon of butter and sauté the onions until they are soft and translucent. Remove from heat and cool.
2. To the bowl of the stand mixer, add bread and pour in the milk. Allow to sit for about 5 minutes, until the bread has absorbed the milk. Add the cooked onions, ground chuck, ground veal, egg, nutmeg, salt and pepper.
3. Tilt motor head back and place the bowl securely on clamping plate. Insert flat beater onto the shaft, make sure that it is hooked properly and place lever on locking position to lock down the motor head completely.
4. Turn the mixer on and set at "SPEED 4" and beat until the mixture is well combined.
5. Turn off stand mixer, place lever on unlock position and lift the motor head to remove the bowl. Form the meat mixture into 1-inch meatballs and place them on a baking sheet.
6. Using the large skillet, melt remaining butter over medium heat. Add half of the meatballs and fry until brown on all sides and cooked through, about 8-10 minutes. Repeat with the second batch.
7. When all meatballs have been cooked, remove them and set aside. To the drippings in the skillet, whisk in the 2 tablespoons of flour. Scrape at all the browned bits until the mixture is brown and frothy. Slowly pour in the broth, stirring to remove any lumps that may form. Cook until it begins to boil and thicken, then pour through a fine mesh strainer to remove any large chunks. Pour the sauce back into the frying skillet.
8. Turn heat to low and stir in the sour cream. Season the sauce with salt and pepper to taste. Return meatballs to the sauce and let simmer until warm, about 5 minutes. Top with chopped parsley and serve over egg noodles or mashed potatoes.

BARBECUE CHICKEN SANDWICHES

For me, the worst part of making barbecue chicken or pork sandwiches is shredding all of the meat. Using your mixer allows you to get dinner on the table that much faster. Prep your sauce while the mixer handles the chicken.

Ingredients:

- 2 chicken breast fillets, boiled or steamed
- Salt and black pepper, to taste
- 1 cup chicken stock

For the Sauce:

- ½ cup barbecue sauce, 1/3 cup ketchup
- 2 tablespoons of light brown sugar
- 2 tablespoons of Worcestershire sauce
- 2 to 3 tablespoons of organic apple cider vinegar
- 2 large shallots, minced
- 1 teaspoon of crushed red pepper flakes or chili powder

Preparation Time: 20 minutes
Cooking Time: 30 minutes
Yields: 4 servings

For Serving:

- 4 slices of sharp white Cheddar cheese
- 4 potato sandwich rolls, sliced into halves
- Sliced red tomatoes(optional)

Directions:

1. In a large pot fitted with a lid, add the stock and apply medium-high heat. Bring to a boil, add the chicken and season to taste with salt and pepper. Cover with lid and cook until it returns to a boil. Reduce to low heat and simmer for about 15 to 20 minutes, or until tender.
2. While cooking the chicken, mix together all sauce ingredients in the mixing bowl. Set aside.
3. When the chicken is done, discard cooking liquid and place the chicken in the mixer bowl. Return the pan to the stove and pour in the sauce mixture. Apply medium heat and cook until it starts to simmer while stirring occasionally.
4. While simmering the sauce, shred the chicken meat in the stand mixer. Tilt stand mixer motor head back and place the bowl securely on clamping plate. Insert flat beater onto the shaft, make sure that it is hooked properly and place lever on locking position to lock down the motor head completely.
5. Turn to "STIR SPEED" and beat for about 30 seconds. Gradually turn to "SPEED 4" and beat until the chicken is shredded evenly. Turn off stand mixer.
6. When the sauce is done, remove from heat and add to the shredded meat. Set to "STIR SPEED" and beat until the meat is evenly coated with the sauce.
7. Turn off mixer, place lever on unlock position and lift the motor head to remove the mixer bowl.
8. Place the bottom slice of each potato roll on a flat work surface and place one slice of cheddar on each potato roll. Top with shredded chicken barbecue and tomatoes and cover with the remaining potato sandwich roll.

HOMEMADE BUTTER

Did you know that when whipping heavy cream first it will turn into whipped cream, but if you continue whipping it will turn to butter? If you enjoy doing everything from scratch, this is the recipe for you and it's so simple you may find that you always want to have your own butter on hand.

Ingredients:

- 2 cups of heavy whipping cream
- 1/8 teaspoon of salt

Preparation Time: 15 minutes
Cooking Time: 20-25 minutes
Yields: 20 pieces

Directions:

1. Tilt motor head back and place the bowl securely on clamping plate. Insert flat beater onto the shaft, make sure that it is hooked properly and place lever on locking position to lock down the motor head completely.
2. Add the cream in the mixing bowl and turn to "STIR SPEED" and beat briefly just to combine. Turn to "SPEED 6" and beat until the mixture clings to flat beater.
3. Turn off stand mixer, place lever on unlock position and lift the motor head before removing attachments.
4. Place a strainer on a bowl and pour the mixture to strain excess liquid. Press lightly to drain remaining liquid and rinse with cold running water until the water runs clear.
5. Salt to taste, mixing the salt into the butter well.
6. Form the butter into a round ball or stick, cover with plastic wrap and chill for at least 2 hours before serving.

BUFFALO CHICKEN BITES WITH JALAPENO

Who said the mixer is just for desserts? Let your mixer help you prepare these delicious appetizer bites to serve at your next party.

Ingredients:

Preparation Time: 15 minutes
Cooking Time: 20-25 minutes
Yields: 20 pieces

- 1 sheet of packaged or prepared puff pastry
- 2 oven-roasted chicken breasts, deboned and cut into quarters
- 1 cup shredded Swiss cheese

For the Sauce:

- ½ cup of red hot buffalo wing sauce
- ½ cup tomato sauce
- 1 large pinch of fine salt
- ½ teaspoon of garlic powder
- 1 green jalapeno, chopped
- 2 medium stems of green onions, chopped
- ½ cup shredded Swiss cheese

Directions:

1. Thaw puff pastry if frozen and preheat your oven to 350°F. Whisk together all sauce ingredients in a mixing bowl until well combined and set aside.
2. Place the chicken meat in the mixer bowl. Tilt motor head back and place the bowl securely on clamping plate. Insert flat beater onto the shaft, make sure that it is hooked properly and place lever on locking position to lock down the motor head completely.
3. Set to "STIR SPEED" and beat for 1 minute. Gradually turn to "SPEED 2" and beat until the meat is shredded evenly. Add in the sauce mixture, turn to "STIR SPEED" and beat until the meat is evenly coated with the sauce.
4. Turn off stand mixer, place lever on unlock position and lift the motor head. Remove bowl and set aside.
5. After thawing the pastry, lay it flat on a floured work surface and spread the chicken mixture evenly on top. Carefully lift the bottom corners of the pastry and gently roll upwards to form into a log. Cut into 1-inch rounds, place it on a floured baking sheet and top with remaining shredded cheese on top.
6. Bake it in the oven for about 20 to 25 minutes, or until lightly browned and the cheese has melted evenly. Remove from the oven, transfer to a wire rack and let sit for 5 minutes before serving.

BACON AND CHEDDAR MASHED POTATOES

Mashed potatoes and then a little extra! These potatoes taste kind of like twice-baked potatoes without the hassle of scooping all the flesh from the skin of the potato.

Preparation Time: 20 minutes
Cooking Time: 20-25 minutes
Yields: 4-6 servings

Ingredients:

- 2 pounds of Vivaldi or Melody potatoes, peeled and quartered
- ½ cup warm whole milk
- ½ cup of shredded Cheddar cheese, plus some for topping
- ½ cup light sour cream
- Salt and black pepper, to taste
- 2 medium stems of green onions, chopped for serving (optional)
- 2 tablespoons of crispy bacon bits, for serving

Directions:

1. In a large pot with boiling water, add the potatoes and cook until tender. Drain potatoes and transfer in the mixer bowl.
2. Cook the bacon until brown, and crisp in a pan over medium-high heat. Transfer to a plate with paper towels, let it rest to cool and chop into fine dices. Set aside.
3. Tilt motor head back and place the bowl securely on clamping plate. Insert flat beater onto the shaft, make sure that it is hooked properly and place lever on locking position to lock down the motor head completely.
4. Set to "STIR SPEED", beat the potatoes for 1 minute and stir in the milk. Turn to "SPEED 2" and beat further until the milk is evenly distributed. Stir in the sour cream and cheese, gradually turn to "SPEED 4"and beat until well combined.
5. Season to taste with salt and pepper, scrape down the sides of the bowl and turn to "SPEED 6". Beat until smooth and fluffy.
6. Turn off stand mixer, place lever on unlock position and lift the motor head. Remove mixer bowl, scrape down the sides and transfer into individual serving bowls or plates.
7. Serve warm with extra shredded cheese, crispy bacon bits and green onions on top.

GARLIC CHEESE BALL

Cheese balls seem to be a staple at holiday gatherings. I like to chill mine for at least 2 hours before serving to make sure everything is well set.

Ingredients:

Preparation Time: 5 minutes
Chill Time: 1 hour
Yields: 1 cheese ball

- 1 teaspoon of finely minced garlic
- ½ teaspoon garlic powder
- 1 ½ cups softened cream cheese
- ¼ cup light sour cream
- ¼ cup grated Parmesan cheese
- ¼ cup shredded Mozzarella cheese
- 1 teaspoon of Italian seasoning mix
- ¼ cup toasted pecans, chopped

Directions:

1. Tilt motor head back and place the bowl securely on clamping plate. Insert flat beater onto the shaft, make sure that it is hooked properly and place lever on locking position to lock down the motor head completely.
2. Place the sour cream and cream cheese in the mixer bowl. Gradually turn to "SPEED 2" and beat until well combined. Add in the cheeses, garlic and Italian seasoning mix while beating constantly until the ingredients are evenly distributed. Scrape down the sides and beat until well incorporated.
3. Turn off stand mixer, place lever on unlock position and lift the motor head. Remove bowl from stand mixer, cover with plastic wrap and chill until set.
4. Form the cheese mixture into a large ball, place the pecans in a large plate and roll the cheese until evenly covered with nuts.
5. Cover with plastic wrap and chill for at least 30 minutes before serving.

CREAMY MASHED POTATOES

A quick and easy way to make mashed potatoes is to let your mixer do a little work. Adjust the butter and milk to your liking. Depending on how long you mix them you can make your potatoes smooth or chunky, whatever your family prefers.

Ingredients:

- 2 pounds Russet or large potatoes, peeled and cubed
- ½ cup of whole milk
- ¼ cup garlic and herb butter
- 1 teaspoon of fine sea salt
- 1 large pinch of ground black pepper

Preparation Time: 15 minutes
Cooking Time: 20-25 minutes
Yields: 4-6 servings

Directions:

1. In large pot with boiling water, add the potatoes and cook until tender. Drain and set aside.
2. Tilt motor head back and place the bowl securely on clamping plate. Insert flat beater onto the shaft, make sure that it is hooked properly and place lever on locking position to lock down the motor head completely.
3. Place the potatoes, set to "STIR SPEED" and beat for about 2 minutes. Gradually turn to "SPEED 2" and beat for about 30 seconds. Add in the remaining ingredients, turn to "SPEED 4" and beat for about 30 seconds.
4. Stop and scrape down the sides of the bowl. Gradually turn to "SPEED 6" and beat until smooth and fluffy.
5. Turn off stand mixer, place lever on unlock position and lift the motor head. Remove from the mixer bowl, transfer to a serving bowl or plates and serve warm.

CHEDDAR CHEESE BALL WITH CRANBERRY AND PECAN

The sharpness of the cheddar seems to accentuate the sweetness of the cranberry in this easy-to-make cheese ball. The pecan adds a bit of necessary crunch. Serve with pita chips or crackers.

Preparation Time: 5 minutes
Chill Time: 1 hour
Yields: 1 cheese ball

Ingredients:

- ½ cup toasted, unsalted pecans
- 1 cup softened cream cheese
- 1 cup shredded sharp Cheddar cheese
- 1 large pinch of salt
- 1 teaspoon of Worcestershire sauce
- 1 to 1 ½ cups of dried cranberries

Directions:

1. Tilt motor head back and place the bowl securely on clamping plate. Insert flat beater onto the shaft, make sure that it is hooked properly and place lever on locking position to lock down the motor head completely.
2. Add butter and cream cheese in the mixer bowl, turn to "SPEED 4" and beat until well combined. Mix in the pecans, Worcestershire sauce and salt, then beat further for 1 minute until well incorporated.
3. Turn off stand mixer, place lever on unlock position and lift the motor head before removing attachments. Remove the bowl from the stand mixer, scrape down the sides and form the mixture into a large ball.
4. Cover the ball with plastic wrap and chill for at least 1 hour, or until set. Remove plastic wrap and place it on a plate. Place the cranberries evenly on all sides and press down to secure into the cheese ball.
5. Serve with crackers or keep refrigerated for later.

GUACAMOLE

Even though it's not hard to mix guacamole by hand, using your mixer gets the avocado smooth and creamy, perfect for dipping chips and crackers.

Preparation Time: 15 minutes
Yield: 4 to 6 servings

Ingredients:

- 3 avocados
- 4 cloves garlic, minced
- ½ medium yellow onion, chopped
- 1 medium tomato, chopped
- ¼ chopped cilantro, (more or less to taste)
- juice from 1 lime
- 1 finely seeded and chopped jalapeño pepper, (more or less to taste)
- salt and pepper

Directions:

1. Cut avocados in half and remove the pits. Scoop the avocado from the skin and put in the stand mixer bowl. Add remaining ingredients.
2. Tilt motor head back and place the bowl securely on clamping plate. Insert flat beater onto the shaft, make sure that it is hooked properly and place lever on locking position to lock down the motor head completely.
3. Turn on the mixer and beat at a low speed until guacamole reached the desired level texture. Blend longer for smoother guacamole.
4. Season to taste, adding more salt pepper, cilantro or jalapeño as needed.

SAUSAGE BALLS

I used to always struggle with the consistency of my sausage balls until I started using the mixer to help me mix the ingredients. We love to have these around the holidays as an appetizer or for breakfast.

Ingredients:

- 1 pound of Italian mild ground sausage
- 2 cups sifted biscuit mix
- 1 teaspoon dried parsley
- 1 ½ cups of shredded sharp Cheddar cheese
- ¼ cup whole milk

Preparation Time: 20 minutes
Cooking Time: 20 to 25 minutes
Yields: 6 to 8 servings

Directions:

1. Preheat the oven to 350°F and lightly grease a rimmed baking sheet with oil or butter.
2. Add all ingredients except for the biscuit mix in the mixer bowl. Tilt motor head back and place the bowl securely on clamping plate. Insert flat beater onto the shaft, make sure that it is hooked properly and place lever on locking position to lock down the motor head completely.
3. Set to "STIR SPEED" and beat until well combined. Gradually add in the biscuit mix while beating constantly until well incorporated.
4. Turn off stand mixer, place lever on unlock position and lift the motor head.
5. Shape into 1-inch balls and arrange it on the prepared baking sheet with 2-inch space.
6. Bake it in the oven for about 20 to 25 minutes, or until lightly brown and cooked through. Remove from the oven, transfer into a plate lined with paper towels and let it rest for about 5 to 10 minutes to drain excess oil.
7. Transfer to a serving plate and serve with preferred condiment.

PAN-FRIED ONION DIP

Easy, tasty onion dip, served with Fritos or the chip or cracker of your preference. Serve at room temperature.

Ingredients:

Preparation Time: 10 minutes
Cooking Time: 30 minutes
Yields: 2 cups

For the Onion:

- 2 cups sliced white onion
- ½ cup grass fed butter
- ¼ cup of olive oil
- 1 large pinch of cayenne pepper
- 1 teaspoon of fine salt
- ½ teaspoon black pepper

For the Dip:

- 1 cup softened cream cheese
- ½ cup light sour cream
- ½ cup real mayonnaise

Directions:

1. In a medium sauté pan, apply medium heat and add the oil and butter. Add the onions when the oil is hot and season to taste with cayenne, salt and pepper. Sauté for 5 minutes while stirring occasionally and reduce to low heat. Cook for 15-20 minutes until the onion is soft and nicely browned. Remove from heat, drain excess oil and set aside to cool.
2. Place all ingredients for the dip in the stand mixer bowl. Tilt motor head back and place the bowl securely on clamping plate. Insert flat beater onto the shaft, make sure that it is hooked properly and place lever on locking position to lock down the motor head completely.
3. Set to "STIR SPEED" and beat for about 30 seconds. Gradually turn to "SPEED 6" and beat until thick and smooth. Stir in the onions, scrape down the sides of the mixer bowl and set to "STIR SPEED". Adjust seasonings according to taste, beat for 30 to 60 seconds or until well incorporated.
4. Turn off stand mixer, place lever on unlock position and lift the motor head. Serve immediately in a serving bowl or store in a covered container in the fridge for future use.

HOT BUTTERED RUM

This classic holiday cocktail is both sweet and slightly spicy. It's perfect to serve at a holiday gathering or on a chilly night cozied up by the fireplace.

Ingredients:

Preparation Time: 10 minutes
Yields: 4 servings

- ¾ cup of spiced rum
- 2 cups boiling water
- 4, 2-inch cinnamon sticks, for serving

Flavoring Ingredients:

- ¼ cup light brown sugar
- ½ cup dark brown sugar
- ½ cup softened butter
- ¼ cup of raw honey
- 1 teaspoon cinnamon powder
- 1 large pinch of nutmeg powder
- 1 small pinch of clove powder
- 1 small pinch of salt

Directions:

1. Place all flavoring ingredients in the mixer bowl. Tilt motor head back and place the bowl securely on clamping plate. Insert flat beater onto the shaft, make sure that it is hooked properly and place lever on locking position to lock down the motor head completely.
2. Gradually turn to "SPEED 4" and beat until smooth and the sugar is dissolved completely. Add in the spiced rum and boiling water, and then beat the mixture on "STIR SPEED" until well incorporated or the butter is fully melted.
3. Turn off stand mixer, place lever on unlock position and lift the motor head. Remove the bowl from stand mixer,
4. Portion hot spiced rum in individual mugs and serve with cinnamon sticks.

PARMESAN AND THYME CRACKERS

These are quite simply delicious. They have the appearance of cookies but are so savory. Serve them with a glass of wine or have them handy for a cheese plate.

Ingredients:

- ½ cup softened butter (unsalted)
- 1 cup Parmesan cheese, finely grated
- 1 ¼ cups sifted plain flour
- ½ teaspoon salt
- ½ teaspoon of ground white pepper
- 1 teaspoon of finely minced fresh thyme

Preparation Time: 15 minutes
Cooking Time: 20-25 minutes
Yields: 30 to 36 crackers

Directions:

1. Mix together the flour, salt and white pepper in mixing bowl until well combined. Set aside.
2. Place butter in the mixer bowl. Tilt motor head back and place the bowl securely on clamping plate. Insert flat beater onto the shaft, make sure that it is hooked properly and place lever on locking position to lock down the motor head completely.
3. Gradually turn to "SPEED 4" and beat until smooth and creamy. Mix in the Parmesan cheese and thyme, gradually turn to "SPEED 6" and beat until well combined.
4. Turn to "SPEED 4", scrape down the sides of the bowl and gradually add in the flour mixture while beating constantly until smooth and well incorporated.
5. Turn off the stand mixer, unlock the motor head and tilt it back to remove the bowl. Transfer dough to a floured work surface and roll out to form a 12-inch log. Cover with plastic wrap and chill for about at least 30 minutes, or until firm.
6. While chilling the dough, preheat your oven to 350°F and lightly dust a baking sheet with flour. When the dough is ready, transfer it to a cutting board and cut into ½-inch rounds. Transfer to the prepared baking sheet and bake for about 20 to 25 minutes, or until lightly golden and crisp.
7. Remove from the oven, transfer to a wire rack and let it rest for about 5 to 10 minutes to cool completely. Serve immediately or store in covered jars for 1 to 3 weeks before serving.

GRAHAM CRACKER CRUSTED PEANUT BUTTER PIE

Graham cracker pies are some of my favorite and this is no exception. You can use your mixer to make fresh whipped cream before assembling the rest of the ingredients. This is a smooth and dreamy pie best served very cold.

Preparation Time: 20 minutes
Cooking Time: 5 to 6 minutes
Yields: 8-10 Servings

Ingredients:

- 1 ½ cups crushed graham crackers
- ¼ cup of melted butter
- 1 cup of whipped cream
- 1 cup softened cream cheese
- 1 ½ cups smooth peanut butter
- ½ cup brown sugar
- 2 teaspoons of vanilla extract

Directions:

1. Preheat your oven to 350°F.
2. Tilt motor head back and place the bowl securely on clamping plate. Insert flat beater onto the shaft, make sure that it is hooked properly and place lever on locking position to lock down the motor head completely.
3. Place the crushed graham and butter into the bowl, set to "STIR SPEED" and beat until well combined. Turn off stand mixer, lift motor head and remove the mixture from the bowl. Press into a 9-inch pie plate and bake it in the oven for about 5 to 6 minutes, or until golden brown. Remove from the oven and set aside to cool.
4. Wipe the bowl and flat beater with cloth and reattach into the stand mixer. Place the cream cheese, peanut butter, sugar and vanilla extract into the bowl. Set to "SPEED 6" and beat until the mixture is thick and smooth. Turn off stand mixer, unlock the motor head and tilt it back to remove the bowl.
5. Place the whipped cream in a separate mixing bowl and gently fold in cheese mixture with a spatula until well incorporated. Spoon mixture into the prepared pie plate and smooth the top with the spatula.
6. Cover with plastic wrap and chill for up to 2 hours before serving.

Dough Hook Recipes

BASIC PIZZA DOUGH

Whenever I think of homemade pizza dough, an Italian chef tossing large circles of dough into the air comes to my mind. But fresh dough is closer, and easier than you think. This recipe yields 2 crusts, so load up on your favorite toppings and invite friends and family over for a memorable homemade pizza night!

Preparation Time: 1 hour
Cooking Time: 10 to 15 minutes
Yields: 2 pizza crusts

Ingredients:

- 3 cups of sifted plain flour
- 2 ¼ teaspoons of active dry yeast
- 1 tablespoon of extra-virgin olive oil
- 2 small pinches of fine salt
- 1 ¼ cups of warm water
- Cornmeal, as needed for dusting

Directions:

1. In a bowl with 1 cup warm water, add in the yeast and stir to dissolve completely. Cover bowl with kitchen cloth and let it stand for 10 minutes for the yeast to activate.
2. Transfer activated yeast mixture to the mixer bowl, together with the oil and salt.
3. Tilt motor head back and place the bowl securely on clamping plate. Insert flat beater into the shaft, make sure that it is hooked properly and place lever on locking position to lock down the motor head completely.
4. Turn to "STIR SPEED" and beat for 30 seconds until the salt is fully dissolved. Gradually add in the flour, beating constantly until well combined.
5. Gradually turn to "SPEED 2" and beat until smooth and elastic, or until the mixture comes together. Add more flour if the mixture is too wet and sticks in the mixer bowl. If the mixture is too dry, add more water until the desired texture is achieved.
6. When the dough is manageable enough, switch the flat beater attachment to the dough hook. Beat for another 8 minutes to knead the dough. Turn off the stand mixer and unlock motor head to remove the bowl.
7. Transfer the dough into a floured work surface and divide into two portions. Roll out each portion to form a ball and transfer to separate bowls greased with oil. Cover with kitchen cloth and let it rise for about 40 to 50 minutes.
8. Return the dough to the floured work area and punch down to remove the air. Gently shape each dough ball into a circle and briefly stretch the sides in circular motion to form pizza crust. Transfer to a pizza stone or baking sheet that is dusted with cornmeal.
9. Top with preferred toppings and sauce and bake it in the oven at 400°F for 10 to 15 minutes, or until golden brown.

FRENCH BREAD

French bread is so versatile. A crunchy crust and a soft center make this the perfect loaf to make for sandwiches, serve with a bowl of soup or use in other recipes.

Ingredients:

- 2 teaspoons of active quick-rise dry yeast
- 4 cups unbleached bread flour, sifted
- 2 teaspoons of salt
- 1 ½ cups of warm water

Preparation Time: 2 hours
Cooking Time: 20-25 minutes
Yields: 2 loaves

Directions:

1. Reserve ¼ cup flour and set aside. This will be used, if needed to thicken the dough later.
2. Tilt motor head back and place the bowl securely on clamping plate. Insert flat beater onto the shaft, make sure that it is hooked properly and place lever on locking position to lock down the motor head completely.
3. In the mixer bowl, add the remaining flour, salt on one side of the bowl and yeast on the other side. Pour in the warm water, turn to "STIR SPEED" and beat until the mixture is smooth and forms into a manageable dough.
4. Switch the flat beater for the dough hook. Gradually turn to "SPEED 2" and beat for 3 minutes to knead the dough until it doesn't stick on the side of the bowl. Add more flour if the mixture is too wet and add more water if too dry.
5. Let the dough rest for 5 minutes and knead again for another 3 minutes on "SPEED 2". Turn off stand mixer and transfer the dough to a floured work surface.
6. Briefly knead the dough and form into a ball. Transfer to a well-oiled bowl, turn the dough over to coat evenly with oil and cover with kitchen cloth. Let it rise for 1 ½ hours or until it has doubled in size.
7. After 1 hour of rising the dough, preheat the oven to 450°F and place a large baking sheet without a rim in the oven.
8. When the dough has doubled in size, return to the floured work surface and punch down to remove some air inside. Roll out to form into a ball and divide dough in half.
9. Form each ball into a long log shape.
10. Remove the heated baking sheet from the oven and sprinkle with cornmeal or flour. Place the log shaped dough on the baking sheet. Make shallow diagonal cuts on top with a knife.
11. Place the dough in the oven and bake it for 20 to 25 minutes or until golden brown. Remove from the oven, transfer to a wire rack and let it rest to cool completely before slicing.
12. Slice with a serrated knife and serve.

CINNAMON ROLLS

Make mornings delicious with these mouth-watering cinnamon rolls. To prepare the rolls the night before, follow steps 1-5. Then cover the rolls with plastic wrap and place in the refrigerator overnight. In the morning, remove from the fridge, discard plastic wrap and allow to sit at room temperature for about 1 hour to rise. Bake the rolls according to the recipe.

Preparation Time: 1 hour, 15 minutes
Cooking Time: 20 minutes
Yields: 12 rolls

Ingredients:

- 1 cup of warm milk
- 1 large egg, whisked
- ¼ cup of unsalted, melted butter
- ¼ cup of vegetable shortening or oil
- ½ cup granulated sugar
- ½ teaspoon of salt
- 3 ½ cups sifted flour
- 2 teaspoons active dry yeast
- ½ cup of melted butter

For the Cinnamon Mixture:

- ½ cup of granulated sugar
- ½ cup of light brown sugar
- 2 ½ tablespoons of ground cinnamon

For the Frosting:

- ½ cup of softened butter
- ¼ cup softened cream cheese
- 1 ½ cups sifted confectioner's sugar

Directions:

1. Tilt motor head back and place the bowl securely on clamping plate. Insert dough hook onto the shaft, make sure that it is hooked properly and place lever on locking position to lock down the motor head completely.
2. Mix together the egg, milk, oil, butter, sugar and salt in the mixer bowl and place the flour and yeast on top. Gradually turn to "SPEED 4" and beat until the mixture is smooth and the dough comes together.
3. Transfer to a greased bowl, cover with kitchen cloth and let it rise for 1 hour, or until it has doubled in size.
4. While the dough is rising, mix together the cinnamon mixture: cinnamon, white and brown sugar and set aside. Preheat the oven to 375 °F and lightly grease a baking sheet with butter.

5. When the dough has doubled, transfer to a floured work surface and roll out into a 10x10 inch flat rectangle. Sprinkle the cinnamon mixture evenly on top. Roll the dough upwards to form into a log, pinch the edge to seal the roll and cut in half. Divide each half into 6 slices and transfer to the greased baking sheet, with the spiral of cinnamon facing up.
6. Bake it in the oven for about 20 minutes or until golden brown in color.
7. While baking the cinnamon rolls, place all frosting ingredients in the clean stand mixer bowl and attach flat beater in the stand mixer. Gradually turn to "SPEED 6" and beat until smooth and creamy. Turn off stand mixer and remove the bowl.
8. When the cinnamon rolls are done, transfer to a wire rack and let cool. Spread evenly with the frosting and serve immediately.

MILK BREAD

This bread is pillowy and soft with just a hint of sweetness. I love to serve this bread lightly toasted with a thin smear of jam.

Ingredients:

Preparation Time: 2 Hours
Cooking Time: 25 Minutes
Yields: 2-9x5 Loaves

- ¼ cup of granulated sugar
- ½ cup sifted cake flour
- 3 ½ cups sifted, unbleached bread flour
- 2 ¼ teaspoons of instant dry yeast
- 1 ½ teaspoons of salt
- ¾ cup heavy whipping cream
- 1 cup whole milk

For the Egg Wash:

- 1 large whole egg
- 1 teaspoon milk

For the Simple Syrup:

- 1 tablespoon sugar
- 1 tablespoon hot water

Directions:

1. In the mixer bowl, add the flours, egg, milk, cream, sugar, yeast and salt. Tilt motor head back and place the bowl securely on clamping plate. Insert dough hook onto the shaft, make sure that it is hooked properly and place lever on locking position to lock down the motor head completely.
2. Turn to "STIR SPEED" and beat until the ingredients are evenly distributed and well combined. Add more flour if the mixture is too wet and beat until well incorporated and the dough comes together. Allow to knead for about 15 minutes, stopping to scrape down the bowl and adjust dough if necessary.
3. Turn off stand mixer, remove the mixer bowl and cover with a kitchen cloth. Let it stand for about 1 ½ hours in a warm spot until the dough has doubled in size.
4. While the dough is rising, mix together the egg wash ingredients in a small bowl and set aside. In a separate bowl, whisk together all syrup ingredients until the sugar is fully dissolved, set aside.
5. Preheat the oven to 350°F and lightly grease two9x5 bread loaf pans with butter and set aside.
6. Return the mixer bowl with dough in the stand mixer and beat for 5 minutes on "STIR SPEED" to remove the air inside. Transfer to a floured work surface and cut in half. Roll out to form into loaves and place in the prepared loaf pans.
7. Brush with egg wash on top and bake it in the oven for 25 minutes. Remove from the oven and brush with syrup mixture. Transfer to a wire rack and let it rest for 10 minutes before serving.

HONEY WHITE BREAD

The perfect sandwich bread. This is a great recipe for the beginner bread maker. It's easy to follow, contains simple ingredients and creates delicious loaves every time.

Ingredients:

- ½ cup of warm water
- 2 teaspoons of active dry yeast
- 1 teaspoon of granulated sugar
- 1 ½ cups of warm milk
- 1/3 cup of softened butter
- 1 to 2 tablespoons of honey
- 2 large egg yolks
- 5 ½ cups sifted flour
- 2 teaspoons of salt
- 1 large egg white, whisked

Preparation Time: 2 hours, 30 minutes
Cooking Time: 40-45 minutes
Yields: 2-9x5 loaves

Directions:

1. Tilt motor head back and place the bowl securely on clamping plate. Insert dough hook onto the shaft, make sure that it is hooked properly and place lever on locking position to lock down the motor head completely.
2. Add the yeast and sugar with warm water in the mixer bowl and stir until the sugar and yeast are fully dissolved. Let it stand for 5 minutes for the yeast to activate.
3. Mix in the honey, butter and milk and turn to "STIR SPEED". Beat until evenly combined and add the yolks one at a time while beating constantly. Add in the salt and flour, beat until well combined and gradually increase to "SPEED 2".
4. Beat until the dough doesn't stick on the side of the bowl or until it comes together, about 5-6 minutes.
5. Turn off stand mixer, transfer to a floured work surface and knead briefly to form into a ball. Transfer to well-greased mixing bowl. Cover with cloth and let it rise for 1 to 1 ½ hours, or until it has doubled in size.
6. Lightly grease two 9x5 bread loaf pans with butter and preheat your oven to 350°F.
7. When it has doubled in size, remove from the bowl and transfer to a floured work surface. Cut in half and lightly knead to form each section into a log. Place in the prepared loaf pans, cover with cloth and let it rise for another 1 hour.
8. Brush the top with whisked egg white and bake it in the oven for about 40 to 45 minutes, or until golden. Remove from the oven, transfer to a wire rack and let it rest for at least10 minutes before slicing.
9. Slice and serve.

HONEY WHEAT BREAD

If you like using whole-wheat flour then this is the recipe for you. This bread makes great sandwiches or you can toast it and add a little butter. It's soft and light and the honey adds just the right amount of sweetness.

Ingredients:

Preparation Time: 2 hours
2 hours, 30 minutes
Cooking Time: 30 to 40 minutes
Yields: 2 9x5 loaves

- 2 ½ cups warm water (about 100 -110 degrees F)
- ¼ cup vegetable oil
- 2 tablespoons caramel color
- ½ cup honey
- 3 ½ cups whole-wheat flour
- 2 tablespoons cocoa
- 2 tablespoons active dry yeast
- 1 teaspoon salt
- 2-3 cups bread flour
- rolled oats for garnishing the top of the loaves

Directions:

1. Tilt motor head back and place the bowl securely on clamping plate. Insert dough hook onto the shaft, make sure that it is hooked properly and place lever on locking position to lock down the motor head completely.
2. Add together the water, oil, caramel color and honey in the mixer bowl. Turn to "STIR SPEED" and mix until evenly combined.
3. Add the wheat flour. When that is blended in, add the cocoa, yeast and salt. Continue using "STIR SPEED" until ingredients are well mixed together.
4. Let mixture sit for about 10 minutes. After ten minutes, begin to add the bread flour, one cup at a time until the dough is sticking to the dough hook- about 3-4 minutes.
5. Cover the bowl with plastic wrap that has been sprayed lightly with cooking spray to prevent sticking. Let dough rise for about 30-60 minutes, until doubled in size.
6. Separate dough into 2 pieces. Cover each ball of dough with a piece of lightly sprayed plastic wrap. Sit for 5 minutes. Shape into loaves and place in greased 9x5 loaf pans. Sprinkle lightly with the oats for garnish.
7. Allow to rise for about 30-60 minutes, until doubled again.
8. When the dough is in the final stage of rising, preheat the oven to 350°F. Bake the loaves for 30 to 40 minutes. Serve with butter.

AMISH SWEET BREAD

This is an easy and tasty recipe for the beginner bread maker. It's a dense, but sweet bread and it makes wonderful French toast!

Ingredients:

Preparation Time: 1 hour, 45 minutes
Cooking Time: 30 minutes
Yields: 2 9x5 loaves

- 2 cups warm water (110 degrees F)
- 2/3 cup white sugar
- 1 ½ tablespoons active dry yeast
- 1 ½ teaspoons salt
- ¼ cup vegetable oil
- 6 cups bread flour

Directions:

1. Tilt motor head back and place the bowl securely on the clamping plate. Insert dough hook onto the shaft, make sure that it is hooked properly and place lever on locking position to lock down the motor head completely.
2. Add together the water and sugar in the mixer bowl. Turn to "STIR SPEED" and mix until sugar has dissolved, then add the yeast. Allow to sit about 10 minutes.
3. When yeast starter has formed a creamy mixture with small bubbles, mix in the salt and oil.
4. Using "STIR SPEED" mix in flour one cup at a time. Mix until dough is smooth and non-sticky.
5. Transfer to a large well-oiled bowl, cover with a cloth or light towel and allow to sit until doubled, about 1 hour.
6. Punch dough down. Knead by hand for a few minutes and then separate dough into 2 pieces. Shape into loaves. Grease two 9x5 loaf pans and add the shaped loaves.
7. Allow to rise for about 30 more minutes, until dough has risen about an inch above the top of the pan.
8. When the dough is in the final stage of rising, preheat the oven to 350°F. Bake the loaves for 30 minutes.

ENGLISH MUFFINS

Homemade English muffins are so incredible, you'll never want to eat grocery store muffins again. To get the most nooks and crannies in your muffins, be sure not to over knead the dough. Mix until everything is just blended and you will have muffins with plenty of "fluffiness", perfect for spreading butter or jam.

Ingredients:

Preparation Time: 2½ hours
Cooking Time: 20-25 minutes
Yields: 12 muffins

- 1 cup milk
- 2 tablespoons white sugar
- 1 (.25 ounce) package instant (rapid rise) dry yeast
- 1 cup warm water (120-130 degrees F)
- ¼ cup melted vegetable shortening
- 5-6 cups bread flour
- 1 teaspoon salt
- 4-5 tablespoons cornmeal

Directions:

1. Warm 1 cup of milk in a small saucepan over medium-low heat until it barely begins to bubble. Mix in the sugar so it dissolves completely. Cool until just warm.
2. Dissolve the yeast in warm water and allow to sit for 10 minutes. At this point yeast mixture should be creamy and slightly bubbly.
3. Tilt motor head back and place the bowl securely on clamping plate. Insert dough hook onto the shaft, make sure that it is hooked properly and place lever on locking position to lock down the motor head completely.
4. Add together the yeast, milk mixture, shortening and 3 cups of flour in the mixer bowl. Turn to "STIR SPEED" and mix until smooth. Add salt. Then add the remaining flour, 1 cup at a time until a soft dough is formed. Knead just enough to incorporate ingredients, but don't over mix. This will cause the English muffins to lose their fluffiness.
5. Transfer to a large bowl that has been well-oiled and cover. Allow to rise for about 1 hour.
6. Punch dough down. Roll the dough to half inch thickness. Use a large glass or cookie cutter about 4-5 inches round to cut circles out of the dough. Muffins can be desired size.
7. Place dough circles onto a sheet of wax paper that has been sprinkled with cornmeal. Sprinkle the tops of the muffins with cornmeal as well. Cover loosely and let rise for 1 hour.
8. Grease a large skillet or griddle and warm over low to medium heat. Cook the muffins about 10-15 minutes per side. Allow to cool before storing in a sealed container. Slice right before toasting.

HERB AND CHEESE PULL-APART BREAD

This is one of my favorite breads to serve with dinner. It has so much flavor and is light and fluffy. It's actually very easy to make, but the presentation of the pull-apart bread looks like it was very difficult. This is a great recipe if you want to impress your guests!

Ingredients:

Preparation Time: 2 to 3 hours
Cooking Time: 35- 45 minutes
Yields: 1-9x5 loaf

Bread

- 1 cup warm water
- 3 tablespoons sugar
- 2 ¼ teaspoons instant yeast
- 2 cups bread flour
- 2 tablespoons unsalted butter, melted
- ¾ teaspoon salt
- 1 cup all-purpose flour

Filling

- 4 tablespoons of unsalted butter, melted
- 1 cup shredded cheese
- 1 tablespoon minced garlic
- ¾ cup minced herbs, (such as basil, thyme, rosemary)
- salt and pepper

Directions:

1. Tilt motor head back and place the bowl securely on clamping plate. Insert paddle attachment onto the shaft, make sure that it is hooked properly and place lever on locking position to lock down the motor head completely.
2. Add the water, sugar and yeast in the mixer bowl and stir on low speed until the sugar and yeast are fully dissolved. Then add the 2 cups of bread flour, butter and the salt. Allow to mix until sticky dough is formed.
3. Replace the flat beater for the dough hook. Using "SPEED 2" slowly mix in the all-purpose flour, just a few tablespoons at a time. A thick dough will form. Mix until dough is no longer sticking to the bowl.
4. Turn off stand mixer, transfer to a floured work surface and knead briefly to form into a ball. Transfer to aseparate, greased mixing bowl. Cover with cloth and let it rise for 1 to 2 hours, or until it has doubled in size. Lightly grease a 9x5 bread loaf pan with butter.

5. Punch down the dough and let rest for about 5 minutes on the floured surface.
6. Prepare herb and cheese filling by mixing together the garlic, herbs and cheese. Add salt and pepper, to taste.
7. Roll the dough out so it is about 12x 20 inches. Brush with 2 tablespoons of melted butter. Sprinkle with the prepared herb and cheese mixture.
8. Use a pizza cutter to cut the dough in half lengthwise. Then cut the long strips into 6 pieces each. You will have 12 pieces total.
9. Holding your loaf pan on its short side, so it is tall, stack these squares of dough forming a tower in the loaf pan. This is how the pull-parts are created. If you lose any of the herb cheese mixture just use it as a topping. Drizzle the remaining melted butter on the top.
10. Cover and let rise for about 40 minutes.
11. When the dough is in the final stage of rising, preheat the oven to 350°F. Bake for 35-45 minutes, or until top is golden brown and bread is cooked through. If the top crust begins to brown too quickly you may make a tent of foil.
12. Cool for 20 minutes, before removing from the loaf pan to serving.

PITA BREAD

Pitas make the perfect little pocket for your deli-meat sandwich and homemade pitas are so much better than store-bought. You can make the dough ahead of time and then refrigerate it and use as needed (up to one week.)

Ingredients:

- 1 cup of warm water (around 110°F)
- 1 ½ teaspoons of active dry yeast
- ¼ cup olive oil
- 1 teaspoon of sugar
- 3 cups sifted plain flour
- 1 teaspoon of fine salt

Preparation Time: 2 hours, 30 minutes
Cooking Time: 3-5 minutes
Yields: 8 pitas

Directions:

1. In a small mixing bowl with the warm water, dissolve yeast and sugar completely and let it stand for about 10 minutes for the yeast to activate.
2. Mix together the flour and salt in the mixer bowl with a hand whisk. Tilt motor head back and place the bowl securely on clamping plate. Insert dough hook onto the shaft, make sure that it is hooked properly and place lever on locking position to lock down the motor head completely.
3. Make a well on the center of the mixer bowl and pour in the activated yeast mixture together with ½ cup warm water and 1 tablespoon of oil. Turn to "STIR SPEED" and beat for about 2 minutes. Gradually turn to "SPEED 2" and beat until you have smooth and kneadable dough. Add more flour if the mixture is too wet or add more warm water if too dry.
4. Remove the dough from the stand mixer, dust the bowl lightly with flour and return the dough into the bowl. Turn to "SPEED 2" and beat for about 6 to 8 minutes or until the dough is smooth.
5. Lightly grease separate bowl with oil, place the dough in and cover with a kitchen cloth. Let it rise for about 1 ½ hours or until the dough has doubled in size.
6. When the dough has doubled in size, transfer to a floured work surface and punch down with fist. Knead briefly just to remove the air inside and divide into 8 equal portions. Roll out each portion to form into a ball and transfer to greased baking sheets. Cover with kitchen cloth and let it rise for another 30 minutes.
7. When the dough is in the final rising, preheat the oven to 450°F and dust the work surface with flour. Return the dough to the work surface after the final rising and roll out to form into flat rounds. Return to the baking sheet and brush with olive oil on top.
8. Bake it in the oven for about 3-5 minutes or until lightly golden and the pita has puffed up. Remove from the oven and let it rest for 5 minutes before serving.

BAGELS

Bagels must be difficult to make and should only be attempted by experienced chefs, right? Wrong! If you can boil a pot of water, you can make bagels. And what could be better than a homemade bagel for brunch on a lazy morning? Not much!

Ingredients:

- 1 ½ cups of water
- 1 ½ teaspoons of active dry yeast
- 3 tablespoons of sugar
- 1 ½ teaspoons of salt
- 3 cups of sifted, unbleached bread flour
- 1 teaspoon of ground cinnamon
- 2 teaspoons of roasted garlic (optional)
- 1 tablespoon of sesame seeds (optional)
- Water, as needed for boiling

Preparation Time: 1 hour, 10 minutes
Cooking Time: 30-35 minutes
Yields: 12 Bagels

For the Egg Wash:

- 1 large egg white
- 1 tablespoon of milk

Directions:

1. In a mixing bowl, add warm water and fully dissolve the yeast and sugar. Let it stand for about 5 minutes for the yeast to activate.
2. Tilt motor head back and place the bowl securely on clamping plate. Insert dough hook onto the shaft, make sure that it is hooked properly and place lever on locking position to lock down the motor head completely.
3. In the mixer bowl, mix together 2 cups of flour and salt and make a well on the center. Pour in the yeast mixture, turn to "STIR SPEED" and beat until well combined. Add in the remaining flour and cinnamon while beating constantly until well incorporated. Add more flour if the mixture is too wet or add more water if too dry.
4. Remove the dough from the stand mixer, wipe the bowl with cloth and dust with flour. Return the dough in the mixer bowl and beat for 5 minutes on "SPEED 2" to knead the dough. Transfer to a greased bowl, cover with cloth and let it rise for 20 minutes.
5. Return into the floured work surface and punch down the dough with fist. Knead briefly just to remove the air inside and divide into 12 equal portions. Roll out into small balls and return to the greased baking sheet. Cover with cloth and let it rise again for about 10 minutes.
6. After the final rising, make 2-inch holes by inserting the thumb on each dough and let it stand for another 10 minutes. While dough is resting, preheat your oven to 350°F and bring a large pot with water to a boil. Mix together the egg wash ingredients and set aside.
7. Cook the bagel in the boiling water for about 1 minute and remove with a slotted spoon. Return to the baking sheet, lightly brush with egg wash and top with roasted garlic and sesame seeds, if desired. Bake it in the oven for about 30 to 35 minutes or until golden brown.
8. Remove from the oven, transfer to a wire rack to let cool before serving.

BUTTERMILK BISCUITS

These are tender, fluffy, melt-in-your-mouth biscuits that can be served with anything and they will get gobbled up. The flaky layers are perfect for topping with honey butter, jam or even use them to make the perfect breakfast sandwich.

Ingredients:

- 2 cups all-purpose flour
- 2 teaspoons sugar
- 1 tablespoon baking powder
- 1 teaspoon salt
- 8 tablespoons cold butter, cut into small cubes
- 3/4 cup buttermilk
- 1 egg, beaten

Preparation Time: 20 minutes
Cooking Time: 15 minutes
Yields: 10 to 12 biscuits

Directions:

1. Preheat the oven to 425°F. Grease a baking sheet.
2. Using your stand mixer, tilt motor head back and place the bowl securely on clamping plate. Insert whisk attachment onto the shaft, make sure that it is hooked properly and place lever on locking position to lock down the motor head completely.
3. Using "STIR SPEED" whisk together the flour, sugar, baking powder and salt. Gradually increase the mixer to "SPEED 6" as you slowly add a few cubes of the butter, until the mixture begins to look like cornmeal.
4. Turn off the mixer and replace the whisk attachment with the dough hook. Put the mixer back on "SPEED 6" and very slowly, add in the buttermilk. Stir until the dough just comes together, but don't over mix.
5. Turn off stand mixer, transfer dough to a floured work surface. Use a rolling pin to spread the dough so it is 1 inch thick. Use a circular cookie cutter or a drinking glass to cut biscuits out of the rolled dough. Place biscuit cut-outs onto the prepared baking sheet. Brush the tops lightly with the beaten egg.
6. Bake for 15 minutes or until the tops turn golden brown.

FOCACCIA GENOVESE

Focaccia is a hearty Italian flat bread. It is typically seasoned with olive oil, salt and rosemary. It can be served alongside soup or stew, used as the base for pizza or even as sandwich bread.

Ingredients:

Preparation Time: 2½ to 3½ hours
Cooking Time: 40 minutes
Yields: 1 loaf

- 1 ½ teaspoons of active dry yeast
- 1/3 cup of warm water
- 3 ½ cups sifted plain flour
- 1 ½ teaspoons of fine salt
- 1 ½ cups of water
- 1 ½ tablespoons of light honey
- 1/3 cup of olive oil
- 1 ½ teaspoons of salt
- 2 tablespoons separated leaves of fresh rosemary

Directions:

1. In small bowl, fully dissolve the yeast with warm water and let it stand for 5 minutes for the yeast to activate.
2. Place the bowl securely on clamping plate and insert dough hook onto the shaft. Make sure that it is hooked properly, place lever on locking position to lock down the motor head completely.
3. In the mixer bowl, mix together the salt and flour and make a well at the center. Turn to "STIR SPEED" and gradually pour in the yeast mixture while beating constantly until well combined.
4. Gradually turn to "SPEED 2" and beat until it's both smooth and the dough comes together. Add a bit more flour if dough seems too sticky. Knead the dough for 5-6 minutes.
5. Transfer to a greased bowl, cover with cloth and let it stand to rise for about 2 to 3 hours.
6. When the dough has doubled in size, transfer to a floured work surface and punch down to remove the air inside. Knead briefly and roll out into a rectangle. Transfer to a well-oiled baking pan, cover completely with cloth and let it stand for about 15 minutes.
7. While the dough is resting, preheat your oven to 450°F.
8. When the dough is ready, use your thumb and fingers to press into the dough making indentions all over the top of the loaf. Lightly brush the top with the remaining oil and honey. Sprinkle some salt and top with rosemary. Bake it in the oven for 15 minutes. Reduce oven temperature to 400°F and bake for another 25 minutes, or until lightly golden.
9. Remove bread from the oven, transfer to a wire rack and let it rest for about 10 minutes to cool before slicing. Slice and serve.

BRIOCHE BREAD

Brioche bread is a French pastry bread with a dark golden, flaky crust and a fluffy middle. Due to the large amount of eggs and butter, this brioche practically melts in your mouth.

Ingredients:

- 3 teaspoons of active quick-rise dry yeast
- 1 ½ teaspoons of fine salt
- ½ cup of white sugar
- 4 cups sifted, unbleached plain flour
- 4 eggs
- ½ cup warm whole milk
- 1 cup cubed and softened butter (unsalted)

Preparation Time: 2 Hours, Overnight Chill Recommended
Cooking Time: 30 Minutes
Yields: 2 9x5 Loaves

For the Egg Wash:

- 1 fresh whole egg, 1 medium egg yolk
- 1 small pinch of salt

Directions:

1. Tilt motor head back and place the bowl securely on clamping plate. Insert dough hook onto the shaft, make sure that it is hooked properly and place lever on locking position to lock down the motor head completely.
2. In the mixer bowl, combine together the sugar, yeast, salt and flour and mix until well combined. Turn to "STIR SPEED", add the eggs one at a time while beating constantly until crumbly and gradually pour in the milk. Beat constantly while slowly turning to "SPEED 2" and beat until well combined.
3. Scrape down the sides of the bowl and return to "SPEED 2". Add ¼ cup of butter, one cube at a time while beating constantly until evenly combined and repeat until all of the butter is incorporated. Scrape down the sides regularly to evenly distribute the ingredients.
4. Beat the mixture constantly until smooth and elastic, or until dough comes together, about 3-4 minutes.
5. Remove dough from mixer bowl, transfer to a greased bowl, cover with cloth and let it rise for about 1 ½-2 hours to double in size.
6. When doubled, carefully lift the edges of the dough, where it meets the lip of the bowl. Pull the dough to the center of the bowl, allowing dough to fall back into the bowl in a ball. Cover tightly with plastic wrap and place in the refrigerator. For best results, chill overnight or at least 4-6 hours.
7. Return to a floured work surface, punch down and knead to remove the air inside. Roll out into a log and cut into 12 equal portions. Roll out each portion into a ball and tuck into two9x5 loaf pans, dividing 6 per pan. Allow to rise for another 1-2 hours, until dough looks fluffy and pillow-like.
8. While the dough is in the final stage of rising, preheat the oven to 375°F and whisk together all ingredients for the egg wash in a bowl.
9. When the dough is ready, brush the egg wash on top and bake it in the oven for about 30 minutes until tops are golden brown. Remove from the oven, transfer to a wire rack and let it rest for about 10 minutes to cool before serving.

CHEWY HOAGIE ROLLS

Hoagie rolls are perfect sandwich rolls and have different names depending on which part of the county you are from. Some other names are subs, grinders and heroes. Whatever you call them, these long and narrow sandwich rolls are perfect for toasting and holding your favorite meats, cheeses and veggies.

Ingredients:

Preparation Time: 2 hours
Cooking Time: 20 minutes
Yields: 8 rolls

- 4 cups sifted unbleached, bread flour
- 1 ½ cups of warm water (about 110 to 115°F)
- 2 tablespoons of sugar
- 2 ½ teaspoons of active dry yeast
- 1 teaspoon of fine salt
- ¼ cup cubed unsalted butter

Directions:

1. In a mixing bowl, dissolve the yeast and sugar completely with ½ cup of warm water. Stir and let it stand for 6 to 8 minutes for the yeast to activate.
2. Tilt motor head back and place the bowl securely on clamping plate. Insert dough hook onto the shaft, make sure that it is hooked properly and place lever on locking position to lock down the motor head completely.
3. In mixer bowl, mix together the flour and salt, remaining water and the yeast mixture. Set to "STIR SPEED" and blend ingredients.
4. Gradually add the cubed butter while beating constantly until well combined and the mixture comes together, increasing mixer speed to "SPEED 2." Mix for about 5 minutes, until a soft dough has formed. Transfer to a greased bowl, cover with cloth and let it rise for 1 hour until it has doubled in size.
5. Transfer to a floured work surface, knead briefly and roll out into a log. Cut into 8 equal portions and roll each portion into a small oval. Transfer to baking tray lined with parchment paper, cover and let it rise again for 30 minutes.
6. While the dough is rising, preheat the oven to 375°F. Bake the bread when it has doubled in size. Bake for 20 minutes, or until the top is golden brown.
7. Remove from the oven, transfer to a wire rack and let it rest for 10 minutes before serving.

QUICK AND EASY HAMBURGER BUNS

What's better than perfectly grilled hamburgers for dinner on a summer evening? Hamburgers on homemade buns that only take 40 minutes from start to finish, that's what. This recipe makes 12 buns. If you like sesame seed buns, add a sprinkling on each bun when you apply the egg wash just before baking.

Ingredients:

PreparationTime: 20 minutes
Cooking Time: 8 to 12 minutes
Yields: 12 Buns

- 2 tablespoons active dry yeast
- 1 cup plus 2 tablespoons warm water
- 1/3 cup vegetable oil
- ¼ cup sugar
- 1 large egg
- 1 teaspoon salt
- 3 ½ cups all-purpose flour
- 1 egg and 2 teaspoons water, beaten together

Directions:

1. In a mixing bowl, dissolve the yeast in the warm water. Add the oil and sugar and allow to sit for 5 minutes.
2. Tilt motor head back and place the bowl securely on clamping plate. Insert dough hook onto the shaft, make sure that it is hooked properly and place lever on locking position to lock down the motor head completely.
3. Turn the mixer to "STIR SPEED" and add the egg, salt and flour, 1 cup at a time until a soft dough has formed. Allow dough hook to work the dough for about 3 minutes.
4. Turn off the mixer and remove the dough from the bowl. Divide into 12 equal portions and form into ball/ bun shapes. Place on a greased baking sheet. Cover lightly and allow to rise for about 10 minutes. Preheat the oven to 425°F.
5. Brush the bun tops lightly with the egg and water mixture.
6. Bake the buns for 8-12 minutes or until the tops are golden brown. Remove from oven and place on wire rack to cool before slicing and serving.

BUTTER ROLLS

These delicious rolls are just like Grandma used to make! This book just wouldn't have been complete without a great recipe for butter rolls. It's a crowd pleaser.

Ingredients:

- 1 cup of warm whole milk
- ¼ cup softened butter
- ¼ cup of granulated sugar
- 1 teaspoon of fine salt
- 3 teaspoons of active dry yeast
- 1 teaspoon of granulated sugar
- ½ cup of warm water (around 110°F to 115°F)
- 3 ½ cups of sifted, unbleached bread flour
- 1 large beaten egg
- Extra flour, for dusting

Preparation Time: 1 hour, 15 minutes
Cooking Time: 15 - 17 minutes
Yields: 18 rolls

Directions:

1. Tilt motor head back and place the bowl securely on clamping plate. Insert dough hook onto the shaft, make sure that it is hooked properly and place lever on locking position to lock down the motor head completely.
2. In the mixer bowl with warm water, fully dissolve the yeast and sugar and let it stand for 10 minutes for the yeast to activate.
3. Place the milk in a saucepan over medium heat and cook until it starts to bubble. Transfer to a mixing bowl and melt in the butter and salt. Stir and let it stand to lower in temperature, around 110°F.
4. Add milk mixture, 2 cups of flour and egg in the mixer bowl, turn to "STIR SPEED" and beat mixture for 1 minute. Gradually add in the remaining flour, turn to "SPEED 2" and beat continuously until smooth and it comes together.
5. Beat for 5 more minutes to knead the dough, adding just a bit more flour if dough seems too sticky. Transfer to a greased bowl, cover with cloth and let it stand to rise for about ½ hour, or until it has doubled in size.
6. While the dough is rising, line a baking sheet with parchment paper and set aside.
7. Return the dough to a floured work surface and punch down to remove the air. Cut in three equal portions and roll out into long logs. Cut each portion into 6 equal sections and roll out to form into balls. You should have 18 rolls. Arrange on the prepared baking sheet, cover with cloth and let rise again for another 30 minutes.
8. When the dough is in the final stage of rising, preheat the oven to 350°F. Bake the dough for about 15 to 17 minutes or until lightly golden.

CIABATTA (ITALIAN WHITE BREAD)

This crusty, rustic bread is perfect for dipping in olive oil or serving with a bowl of hot soup. It does require a sponge, or starter, but it is simple and easily pulled together.

Ingredients:

Preparation Time: 4 hours, plus overnight for starter
Cooking Time: 20 minutes
Yields: 2 loaves

For Sponge:

- 1/8 teaspoon active dry yeast
- 2 tablespoons warm water
- 1/3 cup warm water
- 1 cup bread flour

To make Bread:

- ½ tablespoon of active dry yeast
- 2 tablespoons warm milk
- 2/3 cup warm water
- 1 tablespoon olive oil
- 2 cups bread flour
- 1 ½ teaspoon of fine salt

Directions:

1. Make the sponge one day before you plan to make the bread: In small mixing bowl, dissolve 1/8 teaspoon of yeast completely with 2 tablespoons of warm water and let it stand for about 5 minutes for the yeast to activate. Mix together yeast mixture, 1/3 cup water and the flour and stir for 4 minutes. Cover with plastic wrap and allow to stand at room temperature for 12-24 hours.
2. To make the bread: In the stand mixer bowl, combine the ½ tablespoon of active dry yeast and the milk. Stir and let stand for 5 minutes. Tilt motor head back and place the bowl securely on clamping plate. Insert dough hook onto the shaft, make sure that it is hooked properly and place lever on locking position to lock down the motor head completely.
3. Add to the yeast mixture the sponge, flour, water and oil. Turn to "STIR SPEED" and beat constantly until mixture is moistened. Turn to "SPEED 2", add in the salt and beat constantly for about 8 minutes. Transfer to a greased bowl. Cover with cloth and let it rise for about 1 ½ hours, or until it has doubled in size.
4. Transfer the dough to a floured work surface and divide in two sections. Roll out to form into a loaf about 9 inches long and transfer to a greased baking sheet. Give the top of the dough a quick massage with your fingers, to make small indentations in the top and dust lightly with flour.Cover with kitchen cloth and let it stand for another 30 minutes for the dough to rise. Cover loosely and let rise for another 1 ½-2 hours.
5. Place a baking stone into the oven to warm and preheat oven to 425°F when the dough is about halfway through the rise. When dough is almost doubled in size, remove the stone from the oven and carefully transfer the loaves to the warm stone. Bake for 20 minutes or until just beginning to brown.
6. Remove from the oven, transfer to a wire and let it rest for 10 minutes before slicing and serving.

NAAN (INDIAN FLATBREAD)

This flat bread has many uses, such as stuffing with your favorite Indian cuisine, using it to sop up savory sauces or even making a small personal pizza. I typically use a cast iron skillet to cook the bread, but you can also use a grill. Be sure to spray the grates to prevent the naan from sticking.

Ingredients:

Preparation Time: 2 hours
Cooking Time: 6-8 minutes
Yields: 8 servings

- 1 ½ teaspoons of active dry yeast
- ¾ cup of warm water
- ¼ cup granulated sugar
- 3 tablespoons of warm whole milk
- 1 large egg, whisked
- 1 teaspoon of fine salt
- 3 cups sifted, unbleached bread flour
- 1 garlic clove, minced
- ¼ cup of melted butter

Directions:

1. Dissolve the yeast and sugar with warm water in a separate mixing bowl and let it stand for 10 minutes to activate the yeast.
2. Mix together the flour and salt in the mixer bowl and make a well in the center. Tilt motor head back and place the bowl securely on clamping plate. Insert dough hook onto the shaft, make sure that it is hooked properly and place lever on locking position to lock down the motor head completely.
3. Set to "STIR SPEED", add in the yeast mixture together with the egg and milk and beat until well combined. Set to "SPEED 2" and beat until smooth and dough comes together. Transfer to a separate greased bowl, cover with cloth or plastic wrap and let it stand for 1 hour, or until it has doubled in size. Punch down.
4. Transfer the dough to a floured work surface, add in the garlic and briefly knead just to combine. Divide into 8 equal portions, roll out into small balls. Transfer to a greased baking sheet, cover and let rise for another 30 minutes.
5. While the dough is rising, preheat stovetop to medium heat and lightly brush a cast iron skillet with butter. Place the dough on the skillet, lightly press down to flatten and grill for about 3-4 minutes on each side. Brush the top with butter, flip to cook the other side for about 3-4 minutes more. Brush again with butter and cook until done.
6. Cool slightly before serving.

PARKER HOUSE ROLLS

If you want buttery-soft rolls for your family and friends to enjoy, then take the time to try these Parker House rolls. Top with plenty of melted butter and a light sprinkling of sea salt. Serving these at your next special occasion meal may be the start to a yummy, new tradition.

Ingredients:

Preparation Time: 1 hour, 30 minutes
Cooking Time: 10 to 15 minutes
Yields: 2 ½ dozen Rolls

- 2 packages (.25 ounces each) active dry yeast
- 6 tablespoons, plus 1 teaspoon white sugar (divided)
- 1 cup warm water
- 1 cup warm 2% milk
- 2 teaspoons salt
- 1 egg
- 2 tablespoons plus 2 teaspoons canola oil (divided)
- 5 ½ - 6 cups all-purpose flour
- 3 tablespoons butter, melted

Directions:

1. Mix together the yeast, ½ cup of warm water and 1 teaspoon of sugar in the mixer bowl. Allow to sit for about 5 minutes.
2. To the bowl, add the milk, salt, egg, oil remaining water and sugar and 2 cups of flour. Tilt motor head back and place the bowl securely on clamping plate. Insert dough hook onto the shaft, make sure that it is hooked properly and place lever on locking position to lock down the motor head completely.
3. Turn to "STIR SPEED" and beat until evenly combined. Slowly add the remaining flour until a soft dough is formed. Gradually increase to "SPEED 2" and allow dough hook to knead for about 5-8 more minutes.
4. Turn off the stand mixer, unlock lever and lift motor head to remove the bowl. Transfer dough to a greased mixing bowl and cover with kitchen cloth. Let it rise for about 45 minutes or until it has doubled in size.
5. Transfer to a floured work surface and punch down the dough after rising. Divide into two portions, roll out each portion to about a half inch in thickness. Use a 2 ½ inch biscuit cutter to cut the dough. Brush the tops with melted butter.
6. Fold the rolls in half and lightly press the crease to close. Place on a greased baking sheet with about 2 inches between rolls. Cover lightly with towel and allow to rise for 30 minutes.
7. When the dough is in the final rise, preheat the oven to 375°F. Bake the rolls for 10-15 minutes or until the top is golden. Remove from the oven and let rest for 10 minutes before serving.

SOFT PRETZELS

Forget going to the mall when you get a craving for a warm, salty, soft pretzel. Making them in your kitchen is easier than you think. Boiling the pretzels is very simple and will yield the glossy brown exterior with the soft, doughy interior. Sprinkle with coarse salt before baking, or top with a cinnamon sugar mixture for dessert pretzels. What a fun way to make some memories!

Preparation Time: 1 hour, 20 minutes
Cooking Time: 10-12 minutes
Yields: 8 Pretzels

Ingredients:

- 1 ½ cups of warm water
- 1 teaspoon of active quick-rise dry yeast
- 1 tablespoon of white sugar
- 1 ½ teaspoons of fine salt
- 4 ½ cups of sifted plain flour
- ¼ cup melted (unsalted) butter
- Extra coarse salt, for topping

For the Boiling Liquid:

- Water, as needed for boiling
- ½ cup of baking soda

For the Egg Wash:

- 1 large egg yolk
- 1 tablespoon of water

Directions:

1. Mix together the yeast, sugar and warm water in the mixer bowl and stir until the sugar is fully dissolved. Let it stand for about 10 minutes for the yeast to activate.
2. Tilt motor head back and place the bowl securely on clamping plate. Insert dough hook onto the shaft, make sure that it is hooked properly and place lever on locking position to lock down the motor head completely.
3. Set to "STIR SPEED, gradually add in the flour and salt while beating constantly until well combined. Add in the butter, set to "SPEED 2" and beat until well incorporated. Beat for another 5 minutes or until the dough is smooth and it comes together.
4. Transfer the dough to a greased bowl, cover with cloth and let it rise for about 1 hour to double in size.
5. While the dough is almost done rising, fill a large pot with water together with baking soda and bring to a boil. Place 2 sheets of parchment paper near the pot of boiling water. Line 2 baking sheet with parchment paper, brush with oil and set aside. Preheat the oven to 450°F.

6. Lightly grease a work surface with oil and place the dough on it. Cut the dough into 8 equal portions and roll out to form into long thick sticks. Form each stick in a U shape and cross both ends towards the center. Pinch to secure the ends, repeat procedure with the remaining dough and transfer to the prepared parchment paper near the pot.
7. Boil one pretzel at a time for about 30 seconds, remove with a slotted spoon and place on the parchment paper near the stove. Repeat with the remaining pretzels.
8. Let drain completely and transfer to the prepared baking sheet. Lightly brush with egg wash and sprinkle with coarse salt on top. Bake it in the oven for about 10 to 12 minutes or until golden brown. Remove from the oven, transfer to a wire rack and let cool before serving.

MEDITERRANEAN LOAF

This is an updated version of a Mediterranean olive loaf, that introduces other flavors like sun-dried tomatoes, rosemary and garlic. It is not only tasty to eat, but the colors of the ingredients make for a pretty presentation. I think small slices of this bread paired with a savory spread make a nice party appetizer.

Ingredients:

Preparation Time: 2 hours
Cooking time: 30 to 40 minutes
Yields: 1 loaf

- 1 large pinch of saffron or safflower
- 1 cup of water
- 3 cups sifted whole wheat flour
- 1 teaspoon salt
- 1 teaspoon of powdered sugar
- 2 teaspoons of active dry yeast
- 2 tablespoons garlic-infused oil
- ¼ cup sliced black olives
- ¼ cup chopped sundried tomatoes, sliced
- 1 tablespoon chopped fresh rosemary leaves
- 1 teaspoon garlic-infused oil, for brushing
- 2 sprigs of fresh rosemary, for garnish
- Sea salt, for topping

Directions:

1. Soak saffron in 1 cup of warm water for 20 minutes, strain and reserve the liquid.
2. Tilt motor head back and place the bowl securely on clamping plate. Insert dough hook onto the shaft, make sure that it is hooked properly and place lever on locking position to lock down the motor head completely.
3. Whisk together flour and salt. Add to this the yeast, sugar and oil in the mixer bowl. Set to "STIR SPEED", gradually add in the reserved liquid while beating constantly until well combined and add the oil. Turn to "SPEED 2" and beat until smooth and it comes together (about 3-5 minutes).
4. Transfer to a greased bowl, cover with plastic wrap or cloth and let it stand to rise for about an hour, or until it has doubled in size. Punch down.
5. Lightly flour the mixer bowl, return the dough together with the tomatoes, olives and rosemary. Beat for 3 to 4 minutes on "SPEED 2" until smooth and well incorporated.
6. Transfer to a floured work surface and roll out into a loaf. Transfer to a greased baking sheet, lightly brush with garlic oil and press the rosemary leaves evenly on top. Sprinkle with sea salt. Cover with plastic wrap and let it rise for another 30 minutes.
7. Preheat your oven to 425°F while the dough is rising. Bake it for 30 to 40 minutes or until lightly golden and bottom gives a hollow sound when tapped with your knuckle.
8. Remove from the oven, transfer to a wire rack and let it rest to cool before slicing and serving.

Wire Whip Recipes

CREAM CHEESE FROSTING

This is a classic frosting everyone should know how to make. Use it to frost carrot cake, red velvet cake and it is delicious as icing for brownies.

Preparation Time: 10 minutes
Yields: 2 cups

Ingredients:

- 1 cup of softened cream cheese
- ½ cup softened butter
- ½ teaspoon pure vanilla extract
- 1 to 1 ½ cups confectioner's sugar

Directions:

1. Place the butter, cream cheese and vanilla extract in the stand mixer bowl and set aside.
2. Tilt motor head back and place the bowl securely on clamping plate. Insert flat beater onto the shaft, make sure that it is hooked properly and place lever on locking position to lock down the motor head completely.
3. Turn to "SPEED 6" and beat for about 1 minute, or until well combined. Gradually add in the sugar while beating constantly until well incorporated.
4. Turn off stand mixer, place lever on unlock position and lift the motor head before removing attachments. Scrape down the sides of the bowl with spatula and cover the bowl with plastic wrap.

SALTED CARAMEL FROSTING

Let's get indulgent! I LOVE this salted caramel frosting because it's balanced yet has that wow factor that will have the lucky tasters moaning with delight.

Ingredients:

- 1 cup softened butter
- 1 cup of softened cream cheese
- 3 cups confectioner's sugar
- 1 cup salted caramel (ingredients below)

Preparation Time: 25 minutes
Cooking Time: 5 to 10 minutes
Yields: 4 cups

For the Salted Caramel:

- 1 cup packed white sugar
- ¼ cup of warm water
- 1 tablespoon of corn syrup
- ½ cup full cream
- 2 tablespoons of salted butter
- ½ teaspoon of fresh lemon juice
- ½ teaspoon of fine sea salt

Directions:

1. Mix together the water and corn syrup in a medium saucepan and apply medium heat. Cook for 3 minutes while stirring constantly, or until the sugar is dissolved completely. Increase to high heat, cook until the mixture starts to caramelize while swirling the saucepan occasionally.
2. Remove from heat and let it rest for 1 minute to cool. Pour in the cream and stir regularly until evenly combined. Stir in the remaining ingredients and mix until well incorporated.
3. Stir salted caramel mixture constantly for about 10 to 15 minutes until it has cooled completely. Take 1 cup and reserve the rest for future use.
4. Place the butter and cream in the mixer bowl. Tilt motor head back and place the bowl securely on clamping plate. Insert flat beater onto the shaft, make sure that it is hooked properly and place lever on locking position to lock down the motor head completely.
5. Set to "SPEED 6" and beat until the mixture is smooth and creamy. Set to "SPEED 4"and gradually add in the sugar while beating continuously until the ingredients are evenly distributed.
6. Set to "STIR SPEED", slowly add in the salted caramel mixture and beat until well incorporated.
7. Turn off stand mixer, place lever on unlock position and lift the motor head before removing attachments. Scrape down the sides and transfer the mixture into a sealed container before use.

VANILLA BUTTERCREAM FROSTING

The most perfect cake frosting that has both the ability to look beautiful and taste delicious. If you are experimenting with cake decorating, this simple frosting can be dyed any color and used for most any piping.

Preparation Time: 10 minutes
Yields: 2 ½ cups

Ingredients:

- 2 sticks softened butter (unsalted) (1 cup total)
- 3-4 cups powdered sugar
- 2 teaspoons of pure vanilla extract
- pinch of salt
- 2-3 tablespoons milk

Directions:

1. Place the butter in the mixer bowl. Tilt motor head back and place the bowl securely on clamping plate. Insert flat beater onto the shaft, make sure that it is hooked properly and place lever on locking position to lock down the motor head completely.
2. Turn to "SPEED 6" and cream the butter until smooth and creamy, or for about 1 to 2 minutes. Gradually mix in the powdered sugar, about ½ cup at a time. After 1 cup has been added, increase to highest beating speed for about 10-15 seconds. Continue until 3 cups of sugar has been added.
3. Add vanilla and salt and mix until well blended. Add 1 tablespoon of milk at a time and mix well, until desired consistency has been reached. For a firmer frosting, you can add more powdered sugar, for a softer frosting, add more milk.

CHOCOLATE GANACHE FROSTING

This is the most delicious form of frosting that exists for a chocolate lover such as myself. This does not have the sugary, light taste of a milk chocolate frosting. It has much more of the rich, dense flavoring of a bold, dark chocolate. Use it to frost everything!

Ingredients:

- 16 ounces bittersweet chocolate, chopped very fine
- 2 cups heavy cream

Preparation Time: 15 minutes
Yields: 3 ½ cups

Directions:

1. In a medium sized heat-safe sauce pan, over low heat, warm the heavy cream until it just begins to simmer, but don't allow it to boil.
2. Place the chopped chocolate in the bowl of your stand mixer.
3. Pour the warm cream over the top, melting the chocolate. Stir gently to encourage melting. If chocolate does not melt completely, you may blend until smooth, using a food processor or blender. Cool to room temperature.
4. Tilt motor head back and place the bowl securely on clamping plate of your mixer. Insert flat beater onto the shaft, make sure that it is hooked properly and place lever on locking position to lock down the motor head completely.
5. Turn mixer to "SPEED 8" and mix for 2-3 minutes, until frosting become light and fluffy.

COCONUT BUTTERCREAM FROSTING

Coconut buttercream is the perfect frosting to serve on top of pineapple cake or use it to frost cinnamon rolls or cake. You can even add a bit of shredded coconut to the frosting if that is the taste and texture you desire. Be sure to use canned coconut cream and not the coconut milk from the carton.

Ingredients:

- 1 cup of softened butter
- 1 teaspoon of pure vanilla extract
- 3 cups sifted icing sugar
- ½ cup canned coconut cream

Preparation Time: 10 minutes
Yields: 3 ½ cups

Directions:

1. Lift the stand mixer motor head and place the chilled mixer bowl securely on the clamping plate. Insert wire whip properly onto the beater shaft and lock down the motor head completely.
2. Place the butter and vanilla extract in the mixer bowl, gradually turn to "SPEED 2" and beat until well combined. Gradually add in the sugar, slowly increase to "SPEED 8" and beat constantly until well incorporated and soft peaks form.
3. Slowly add in the coconut cream and beat constantly until thick and fluffy.

WHIPPED BROWN SUGAR BUTTERCREAM

Whipped brown sugar buttercream is light and fluffy and has just enough sweetness without being overpowering.

Ingredients:

Preparation Time: 10 minutes
Yields: 2 ½ cups

- ½ cup sifted plain flour
- 1 to 1 ¼ cups whole milk
- 2 ½ teaspoons of vanilla extract
- 1 ½ cup softened butter
- 1 ½ cups packed light brown sugar
- 1 small pinch of salt

Directions:

1. Add the milk to a saucepan and apply medium heat. Slowly add in the flour while stirring constantly and cook until smooth and well combined. Remove from heat, set aside to cool and stir in the vanilla extract.
2. Lift the stand mixer motor head and place the chilled mixer bowl securely on the clamping plate. Insert wire whip properly onto the beater shaft and lock down the motor head.
3. Place the butter, salt and sugar in the mixer bowl and gradually turn to "SPEED 4". Beat until well combined, gradually turn to "SPEED 8" while slowly adding the flour mixture and beat until soft peaks form and it's fluffy.
4. Transfer to a mixing bowl and use immediately as topping. Or cover with plastic wrap and chill before use.

WHIPPED CHOCO-HAZELNUT FROSTING

This light, whipped chocolate frosting has a hint of your favorite hazelnut spread, which sets it apart from most other light chocolate frostings. For best results, chill your mixer bowl for 30 minutes before starting this recipe.

Ingredients:

Preparation Time: 10 minutes
Yields: 1 ½ cups

- ½ cup softened butter
- ½ cup chocolate hazelnut spread
- 1 ½ cups sifted icing sugar
- 1 teaspoon of vanilla extract
- 2 tablespoons of heavy whipping cream

Directions:

1. Lift the stand mixer motor head and place the mixer bowl securely on the clamping plate. Insert wire whip properly onto the beater shaft and lock down the motor head completely.
2. Add the chocolate spread and butter in the chilled mixer bowl. Gradually turn to "SPEED 4"and beat the mixture until it starts to thicken. Scrape down the sides and gradually turn to "SPEED 8" while slowly adding the rest of the ingredients. Beat until well combined and soft peaks form.
3. Turn to "SPEED 4" and beat for about 1 minute, or until smooth and fluffy.
4. Spread evenly on top of the cake or pipe on top of cupcakes.

FLUFFY BOILED ICING

This is an old recipe that creates a tasty sweet frosting with no butter. It is basically made by pouring hot sugar water into beaten egg whites and then beating until a fluffy consistency is reached. This icing is best served right away but can be kept in the refrigerator overnight if needed.

Ingredients:

Preparation Time: 20 minutes
Yields: 2 ½ cups

- 1 ½ cups sugar
- 2/3 cup water
- 1/8 teaspoon cream of tartar
- 3 egg whites
- 1 teaspoon vanilla
- 1 small pinch of salt

Directions:

1. Add the water, sugar and cream of tartar into a saucepan and stir gently. Apply medium heat and bring to a boil. Use a candy thermometer to tell when the mixture has reached 245°F. Do not stir the mixture once you have applied heat as this will cause the mixture to crystallize and you won't be able to use it for the icing.
2. While the sugar mixture is heating, lift the stand mixer motor head and place the mixer bowl securely on the clamping plate. Insert wire whip properly onto the beater shaft and lock down the motor head.
3. Add the egg whites and a pinch of salt and turn mixer to "SPEED 8" and beat egg whites until soft peaks form. Turn off mixer.
4. Carefully pour the hot sugar mixture into the mixer boil, taking care not to splash any of the hot liquid. Turn on the mixer and gradually increase speed to "SPEED 8" and beat for 7 minutes.
5. Add the vanilla extract and beat briefly.
6. Use immediately as the icing does not keep well.

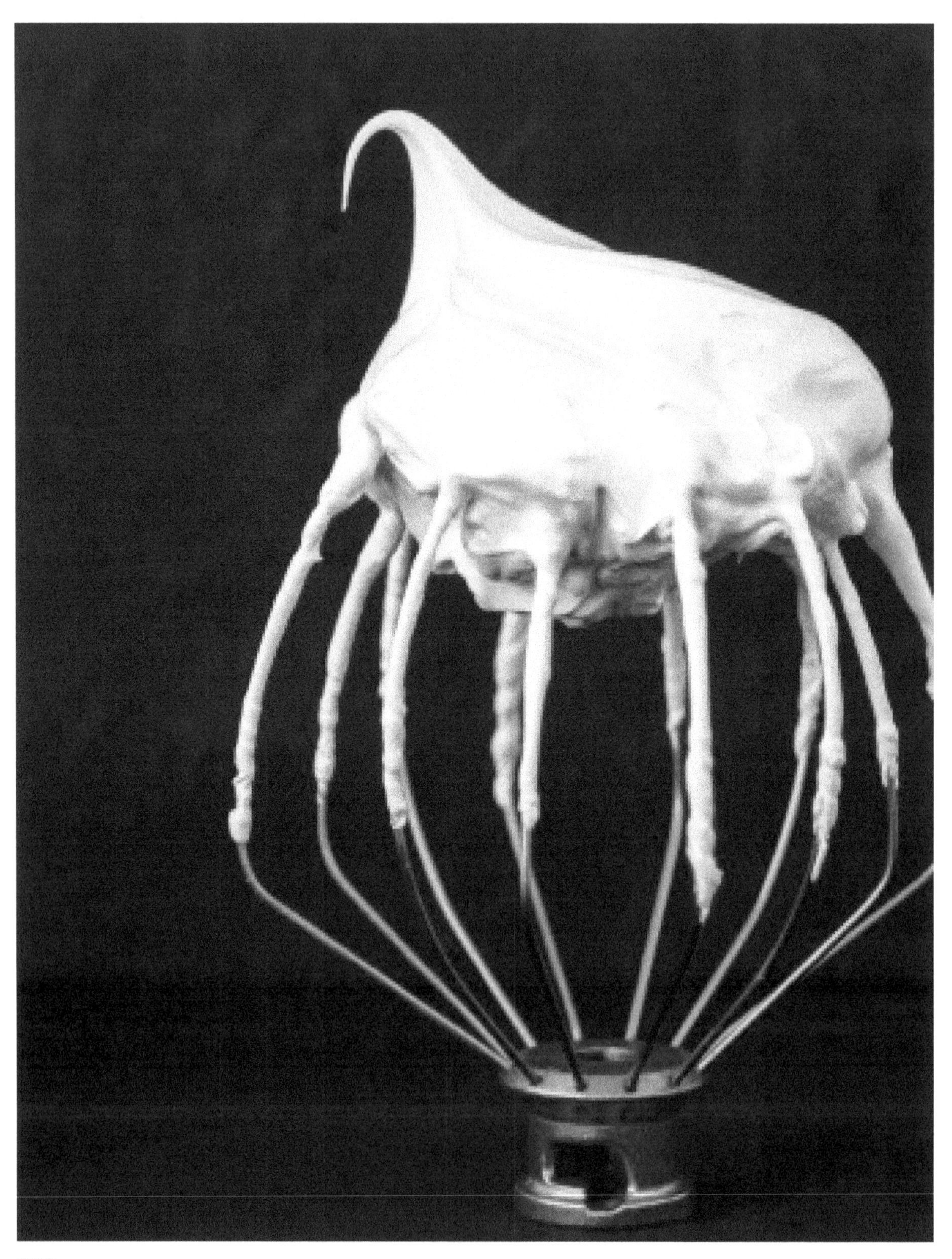

WHIPPED CREAM

Store bought whipped cream will never be allowed in your kitchen after you see how easy and delicious it is to make your own from scratch. For best results, chill your bowl and your whisk before using.

Ingredients:

- 2 cups heavy whipping cream
- 4 tablespoons powdered sugar
- 1 tablespoon vanilla extract

Preparation Time: 10 minutes
Yields: 2 ½ cups

Directions:

1. *It is recommended to place your bowl and your whisk in the refrigerator for about 1 hour before making whipped cream.
2. Lift the stand mixer motor head and place the mixer bowl securely on the clamping plate. Insert wire whip properly onto the beater shaft and lock down the motor head.
3. Add whipping cream, powdered sugar and vanilla into the bowl. Select "STIR SPEED" until ingredients are well incorporated then gradually increase to "SPEED 8."
4. Continue to beat for about 1-2 minutes, being careful not to over beat. Check to see if it is ready by lifting the motor head. If soft peaks have formed on your whisk, the cream is ready.
5. Scoop into a bowl and serve or chill.

STRAWBERRY WHIPPED CREAM

This recipe takes whipped cream to the next level making a whipped cream that can easily be used as a frosting for cakes or desserts. Be sure to use seedless preserves, as the small seeds would ruin the creamy texture of the whipped topping.

Ingredients:

- 1 ½ cups of heavy whipping cream
- ¾ cup of white sugar
- ½ cup seedless strawberry preserves
- 1 small of pinch salt

Preparation Time: 10 minutes
Yields: 2 cups

Directions:

1. *It is recommended to place bowl and your whisk in the refrigerator for about 1 hour before making whipped cream.
2. Lift the stand mixer motor head and place the mixer bowl securely on the clamping plate. Insert wire whip properly onto the beater shaft and lock down the motor head.
3. Place the cream in the chilled mixer bowl, gradually turn to "SPEED 4"and beat until it starts to thicken. Gradually turn to "SPEED 8"and slowly add in the sugar and salt while beating constantly until soft peaks form.
4. Add in half of the preserves and beat on "SPEED 4" until well combined. Add in the remaining preserves and beat on "STIR SPEED" just to fold evenly into the mixture.
5. Serve immediately or chill before use.

FROZEN PEPPERMINT TOPPING

These frozen candies take a bit of time to chill but are the perfect accompaniment to dress up a bowl of ice cream or any chilled dessert. It's also fun to have these around the holidays to put into mugs of steaming hot chocolate. Pipe the whipped cream into any desired shape, add colored sugar if you desire and chill.

Ingredients:

- ¼ cup of sifted white sugar
- 1 ½ cups of heavy whipping cream
- 1 teaspoon pure peppermint extract
- 1 small drop of green food coloring
- 1 tablespoon of colored sugar, for topping

Preparation Time: 20 minutes
Freezing Time: 4 to 5 hours to chill
Yields: 1 ½ cups

Directions:

1. *It is recommended to place bowl and your whisk in the refrigerator for about 1 hour before making whipped cream.
2. Lift the stand mixer motor head and place the chilled mixer bowl securely on the clamping plate. Insert wire whip properly onto the beater shaft and lock down the motor head.
3. Add the cream and sugar into the mixer bowl. Gradually turn to "SPEED 4" and beat the mixture until well combined.
4. Add in the peppermint extract and coloring, gradually turn to "SPEED 8" and beat until soft peaks form and it's fluffy. Line a baking sheet with parchment paper, set aside.
5. Transfer the mixture into a piping bag and pipe into desired shapes on the prepared baking sheets. Top with colored sugar and freeze for at least 4 hours before serving.
6. Remove from the baking sheet, transfer into a sealed container and store it in the freezer for up to 3 weeks.

EASY MERINGUE

This recipe includes instructions for piping the meringue into little individual pieces, but these ingredients can be used to create any sort of meringue topping. Be sure to use room temperature egg whites for the best results. Sitting the egg whites on the counter for 30 minutes prior to whipping them should be sufficient.

Ingredients:

- ½ cup of egg whites
- 1 cup sifted superfine/caster sugar
- 1 teaspoon of pure vanilla extract

Preparation Time: 20 minutes
Cooking Time: 1 hour, 30 minutes
Yields: 18 Pieces

Directions:

1. Preheat your oven to 300°F and line 2 baking sheets with parchment paper. Prepare a piping bag with a star nozzle and set aside.
2. Lift the stand mixer motor head and place the mixer bowl securely on the clamping plate. Insert wire whip properly onto the beater shaft and lock down the motor head.
3. Add in the egg whites in the mixer bowl, gradually turn to "SPEED 8" and beat until stiff peaks form. Slowly add in half of the sugar and vanilla extract while beating constantly until thick and firm. Add in the remaining sugar and beat further until firm and shiny.
4. Spoon the meringue mixture into the piping bag fitted with a star nozzle. Remove the air in the piping bag and pipe the mixture on the prepared baking sheets. Pipe the mixture in a spiral motion until you reach 3 layers. Repeat the procedure with the remaining meringue mixture with 1 to 2-inch spaces.
5. Bake it in the oven for about 1 hour, turn off the oven and let the meringue sit in the oven for another 30 minutes. Remove from the oven, transfer to a wire rack and let it rest to cool before serving or storing in sealed containers.

ANGEL FOOD CAKE

Angel food cake can be a little tricky to get just right, but there are a few rules that make success much easier to reach. Always sift your flour before measuring. Make sure your egg whites contain no yolks and that they are at room temperature. When beating the egg whites, be sure to beat long enough that stiff peaks form. Finally, try to remove any air bubbles from the batter when you pour it into the pan. Follow these few simple rules and you will have a delicious angel food cake to serve friends and family.

Preparation Time: 20 minutes
Cooking Time: 30 to 35 minutes
Yields: one 10 inch cake

Ingredients:

- 1 cup of cake flour, sifted
- 1 ½ cups white sugar, plus 2 tablespoons (divided)
- 12 large egg whites, room temperature
- 1 ½ teaspoons cream of tartar
- ¼ teaspoon salt
- 1 ½ teaspoons of pure vanilla extract
- ½ teaspoon of almond extract

Directions:

1. Preheat your oven to 375°F. You will need a 10-inch tube pan with a removable bottom or an angel food cake pan. Do not use any oil or grease on the pan.
2. In a medium bowl, whisk together 3/4 cup, plus 2 tablespoons of white sugar and 1 cup cake flour. Whisk well to combine the ingredients.
3. To your mixing bowl, add egg whites, cream of tartar and salt.
4. Lift the stand mixer motor head and place the mixer bowl securely on the clamping plate. Insert wire whip properly into the beater shaft and lock down the motor head.
5. Gradually increase your mixer to “SPEED 6” and beat until soft peaks start to form. Add remaining 3/4 cup of white sugar and increase to “SPEED10.” Continue to beat until stiff peaks form.
6. Decrease mixer speed to “SPEED 2” and add the vanilla extract, almond extract and finally, the flour. Mix until well combined.
7. Turn off stand mixer, place lever on unlock position and lift the motor head before removing attachments. Scrape the sides of the bowl and remove from the mixer.
8. Pour half of the batter into the tube pans and smooth with a spatula to remove any air bubbles. Pour the remaining batter and smooth again.
9. Bake it in the oven for about 30-35 minutes. It is done when the cake is springy to the touch
10. Remove from the oven, transfer to a wire rack and let it cool completely before inverting and removing from the pan.

WHIPPED SHORTBREAD COOKIES

Just a few simple ingredients mixed together and the results are a delectable cookie that melts in your mouth. For the lightest, airiest texture for your cookies, whip the butter for about 3 minutes.

For best results, chill your mixer bowl before using.

Ingredients:

Preparation Time: 10 minutes
Cooking Time: 12-14 minutes
Yields: 3 dozen

- 1 small pinch of salt
- ½ cup sifted cornstarch
- 3 cups sifted plain flour
- 2 cups softened butter
- 1 cup sifted powdered sugar
- 1 teaspoon of pure vanilla extract

Directions:

1. Preheat oven to 350°F and line 2 baking sheets with parchment paper. Set aside.
2. Lift the stand mixer motor head and place the chilled mixer bowl securely on the clamping plate. Insert wire whip properly onto the beater shaft and lock down the motor head completely.
3. Add in butter and vanilla in the mixer bowl, gradually turn to "SPEED 4" and beat until the mixture is smooth and creamy. Slowly add in the sugar and salt, gradually turn to "SPEED 6 or 8" and beat until soft peaks form and fluffy.
4. Slowly add in the flour and starch while beating constantly on "SPEED 4" and beat until well incorporated.
5. Transfer the mixture into a cookie press and press out cookie mixture on the prepared sheets. Bake it in the oven for about 12 to 14 minutes.
6. Remove from the oven, transfer to a wire rack and let it rest to cool completely before serving. Or store it in a sealed container for up to 3 weeks for future consumption.

MANGO PANNA COTTA

A tropical twist on an Italian classic. Panna Cotta is like a firm pudding with a silky, smooth texture. It's perfect to serve at a fancy dinner party or just when you want to make your weeknight special.

Ingredients:

Preparation Time: 25 minutes
Yields: 6 to 8 servings

- 1 packet or 1 tablespoon gelatin
- ¼ cup of water (cold)
- 2 cups of full cream
- ¼ cup white sugar
- 2 cups of whole milk
- 1 teaspoon of pure vanilla extract
- 1 large pinch of ground nutmeg
- 1 small pinch of salt
- 3 large ripe yellow mangos, pitted and sliced or cubed

Directions:

1. Dissolve the gelatin in a bowl with water, let it stand for 5 minutes and apply with medium heat. Cook mixture in a saucepan while stirring constantly until the gelatin is fully dissolved. Remove from heat, transfer to a mixing bowl and let it rest to cool.
2. Lift the stand mixer motor head and place the mixer bowl securely on the clamping plate. Insert wire whip properly onto the beater shaft and lock down the motor head.
3. In the same pan, apply medium heat and mix together the cream and sugar. Cook until the mixture starts to simmer while stirring regularly and transfer into the mixer bowl.
4. Gradually turn to "SPEED 2" and beat until the sugar is dissolved completely. Add in the gelatin mixture, vanilla extract, salt and milk, gradually turn to "SPEED 6" and beat until well incorporated and fluffy.
5. Divide the sliced mangos into two equal portions. Portion half of the mangos on 6 ramekins or small bowls and fill with cream-milk mixture. Chill for at least 1 to 2 hours or until the mixture has begun to set. Portion the rest of the mangos on each ramekin and spread evenly on top.
6. Return into the fridge, sprinkle with nutmeg on top and chill until set before serving.

LEMON COOL WHIP COOKIES

This is a simple recipe that utilizes making your own version of Cool Whip topping to make these delicious lemony cookies. These cookies are soft and light and the recipe is quite versatile, too. Use a devil's food cake mix for chocolate cookies or a strawberry cake mix for strawberry cookies. The possibilities are endless!

Ingredients:

- 1 (15 -16 oz.) package of lemon cake mix
- 1 large egg
- ½ cup of powdered sugar, sifted

For the Whipped Cream Topping:

- ¼ cup warm water
- 1 teaspoon unflavored gelatin
- ½ teaspoon cream of tartar
- 1 ¾ cups of heavy whipping cream
- 3 tablespoons of sugar
- 1 teaspoon of pure extract vanilla

For best results, chill your mixer bowl before using.
Preparation Time: 10 minutes
Cooking Time: 10 minutes
Yields: 4 dozen

Directions:

1. In a small saucepan with warm water, fully dissolve the gelatin and let it sit to cool for about 2 to 3 minutes.
2. Lift the stand mixer motor head and place the chilled mixer bowl securely on the clamping plate. Insert wire whip attachment properly onto the beater shaft and lock down the motor head completely.
3. Add the heavy cream in the mixer bowl, turn to "STIR SPEED" and add in the cream of tartar while beating constantly until well combined. Gradually turn to "SPEED 2" and slowly add in the sugar while beating constantly until well combined.
4. Gradually pour in the gelatin mixture and the vanilla extract while beating constantly until well incorporated. Gradually turn to "SPEED 8" and beat until soft peaks form.
5. Preheat your oven to 350°F, lightly grease a cookie sheet with oil and place the caster sugar in a separate medium sized bowl. Set aside.
6. Add the egg into the mixer bowl and beat on "SPEED 2" until well combined. Gradually add in the cake mix while beating constantly until well incorporated.
7. Drop a tablespoon of cookie mixture in the bowl with powdered sugar, coat evenly on all sides and transfer to the prepared cookie sheet. Repeat the procedure with the remaining cookie mixture and place on the sheet 1-2 inches apart.
8. Bake for about 10 minutes, or until the cookies are lightly brown. Remove the cookies from the oven, transfer to a wire rack and cool completely before serving.

HAM AND ASPARAGUS QUICHE

This delicious quiche is the perfect breakfast or brunch food to serve to your special person. Using the stand mixer insures that the egg mixture gets well mixed, resulting in the fluffiest, lightest quiche you've ever tasted. You can even experiment with different flavors by changing up the meat and vegetables in the recipe to your taste.

Preparation Time: 10 minutes
Cooking Time: 30-35 minutes
Yields: 8-10 Servings

Ingredients:

- 1 (9-inch) pre-made/packaged pie crust
- 1 ½ cups grated Swiss or Cheddar cheese
- 3 large whole eggs
- 1 cup whole milk
- ½ cup of full cream
- 1 teaspoon of fine salt

For the Filling:

- ½ cup diced white onion
- ½ pound fresh asparagus, cut into ½-inch pieces
- ½ pound diced smoked ham

Directions:

1. Preheat your oven to 350°F, line a 9-inch pie plate with parchment paper and lightly brush with oil. Roll out the premade pie crust and fit into the prepared cake tin. Press down the bottom and sides.
2. Cover the crust with another piece of parchment paper and fill with dry beans to retain its shape when baking. Bake it in the oven for about 15 minutes, remove beans and parchment paper and bake further for about 10 minutes or until lightly golden. Remove from the oven and let it rest to cool.
3. While baking the crust, sauté the ham and onions in a non-stick skillet until lightly golden. Stir in the asparagus and sauté further until the asparagus is lightly wilted. Remove from heat and set aside.
4. Lift the stand mixer motor head and place the mixer bowl securely on the clamping plate. Insert wire whip properly onto the beater shaft and lock down the motor head. Add in the cream, eggs, milk and salt in the mixer bowl and gradually turn to "SPEED 6". Beat until smooth and frothy.
5. Sprinkle half of the cheese on the bottom of the precooked crust. Add in the sautéed ham, onion and asparagus and distribute evenly on the bottom. Pour the egg mixture into the pie crust and top with the remaining cheese.
6. Bake it in the oven for about 30 to 35 minutes, or until the side is set but the center is still a little runny. Remove from the oven, transfer to a wire rack and let it rest for about 20 minutes before slicing and serving.

FLUFFY CHEESE OMELETTE

Use your stand mixer to fluff the eggs and heavy cream just the right amount to get the perfect fluffy omelet.

Ingredients:

- ½ cup heavy whipping cream
- 3 large whole eggs
- 1 tablespoon ghee/clarified butter
- Salt and black pepper, to taste
- 1 large pinch of mixed Italian herbs
- ¼ cup grated sharp Cheddar cheese

Preparation Time: 5 minutes
Cooking Time: 10 minutes
Yields: 2 Servings

Directions:

1. Lift the stand mixer motor head and place the chilled mixer bowl securely on the clamping plate. Insert wire whip properly onto the beater shaft and lock down the motor head.
2. Place the eggs and cream in the mixer bowl, gradually turn to "SPEED 6" and beat until soft peaks form and fluffy.
3. Add the ghee in a medium skillet, apply medium high heat and season with Italian herbs, salt and pepper. Cook until 75% of the mixture is cooked while stirring constantly with a spatula.
4. Reduce to low heat, top with grated Cheddar cheese and cover with lid. Cook for about 1 to 2 minutes, or until the cheese has fully melted. Remove from heat and serve.

GREEK AVGOLEMONO CHICKEN SOUP

Avgolemono actually means Egg Lemon and that's just what you get with this Greek version of classic, comforting, chicken noodle soup.

PreparationTime: 15 minutes
Cooking Time: 15 minutes
Yields: 4 servings

Ingredients:

- 1 tablespoon of chicken broth base
- 4 cups of chicken stock
- ½ cup raw orzo pasta or long grain rice
- Salt and black pepper, to taste
- 3 large whole eggs
- 1 large organic lemon, juiced
- 1 cup shredded chicken

Directions:

1. Pour the broth in a medium saucepan, apply medium-high heat and bring to a boil. Add in the orzo or rice and cook for about 5 minutes, or until it returns to a boil. Season to taste with salt and pepper, reduce to low heat and simmer while preparing the other ingredients.
2. Lift the stand mixer motor head and place the mixer bowl securely on the clamping plate. Insert wire whip properly onto the beater shaft and lock down the motor head.
3. Add the eggs and lemon juice in the mixer bowl and gradually turn to "SPEED 8" while beating constantly until thick and frothy. Turn to "SPEED 4", stir in about 1 cup of hot broth while beating constantly until well combined.
4. Transfer the mixture into the saucepan and cook until the soup reaches a simmer while stirring regularly. Stir in the shredded chicken and allow to warm.
5. Adjust seasonings according to taste, portion into individual serving bowls and serve immediately.

MAYONNAISE

Homemade mayonnaise is simple when you've got a stand mixer working for you. These simple ingredients blended together make your favorite condiment so much tastier and healthier than you can buy at the store.

Ingredients:

PreparationTime: 10 minutes
Yields: 3 cups

- 2 eggs
- 2 tablespoons Dijon mustard
- 2 and 2/3 cups vegetable oil
- 8 teaspoons white wine vinegar
- salt and pepper to taste

Directions:

1. Lift the stand mixer motor head and place the mixer bowl securely on the clamping plate. Insert wire whip properly onto the beater shaft and lock down the motor head.
2. Add the egg yolk and mustard, gradually turn to "SPEED 2" and beat until well combined.
3. Gradually turn to "SPEED 6" while very slowly adding the oil and beat constantly until all of the oil is well incorporated.
4. Add in the vinegar. Season to taste with salt and pepper.
5. Let it rest for 1 to 2 minutes at room temperature, cover bowl and store in the fridge for up to 4 days.

ICED AMARETTO COFFEE

This is an incredibly delightful little cocktail after a meal on a summer night. After you try it once, it would only surprise me if you don't revisit this one fairly often.

Ingredients:

- 3 tablespoons of instant cappuccino or mocha coffee
- 1 ½ cups of hot water
- ½ cup amaretto cream liqueur

Preparation Time: 5 minutes
Yields: 2 Servings

For Serving:

- Whipped cream
- Sliced almonds or mini chocolate chips
- Ice cubes, for serving

Directions:

1. Lift the stand mixer motor head and place the mixer bowl securely on the clamping plate. Insert wire whip properly onto the beater shaft and lock down the motor head.
2. Add the hot water and instant coffee in the mixer bowl and gradually turn to "SPEED 2". Beat until well combined, add in ½ cup ice cubes to lower temperature and stir in the cream liqueur.
3. Gradually turn to "SPEED 6" and beat until the coffee mixture is smooth and frothy.
4. Fill 2 tall serving glasses with ice cubes and pour in the whipped coffee mixture. Top with whipped cream and almonds or chocolate chips and serve immediately.

HOMEMADE EGGNOG

This quintessential holiday drink can be prepared with the help of your stand mixer. Spike it with rum or cognac to really get the party started!

Ingredients:

- 2/3 cup egg yolk
- ½ cup of white sugar
- 1 cup of heavy whipping cream
- 2 cups of whole milk
- ½ teaspoon of ground nutmeg
- 1 small pinch of fine salt
- ½ teaspoon of pure vanilla extract
- Cinnamon powder, as needed for sprinkling

Preparation Time: 5 minutes
Cooking Time: 10 minutes
Yields: 4 servings

Directions:

1. Lift the stand mixer motor head and place the mixer bowl securely on the clamping plate. Insert wire whip properly onto the beater shaft and lock down the motor head.
2. Add in the yolks and sugar in the mixer bowl, gradually turn to "SPEED 2" and beat until well combined and creamy. Set aside.
3. Combine together the cream, milk, nutmeg and salt in a saucepan and apply with medium-high heat. Cook until it reaches a simmer while stirring constantly and remove from heat.
4. Add 2 tablespoons of hot milk mixture in the mixer bowl while beating constantly. Add in another 2 tablespoons of milk mixture and beat until well combined. Gradually turn to "SPEED 6" and continue the procedure until all of the milk mixture has been added.
5. Beat until well incorporated and frothy, transfer the mixture to a pot and cook until a thermometer registers 160°F while whisking constantly. Remove from heat and stir in the vanilla.
6. Transfer eggnog mixture to a covered pitcher or jar and chill for at least 2 hours before serving. Pour into glasses, sprinkle cinnamon on top and serve.

MOZZARELLA STUFFED MEAT BALLS

Homemade meatballs are even more delicious if you are using the freshest ingredients. Select a quality cut of meat and grind your own beef and pork. Then add seasonings and fresh mozzarella and you have a meal or appetizer that is sure to be a hit at even the fanciest party.

Preparation Time: 25 minutes
Cooking Time: 10 to 15 minutes
Yields: 3 dozen

Ingredients:

- 1 ½ cups cubed Mozzarella cheese
- ½ cup Olive oil
- ½ cup Coconut oil

For the Meatballs:

- ¼ cup finely diced shallots
- ¼ cup canned sun-dried tomatoes, drained
- ¼ cup finely chopped basil leaves
- ¼ cup grated Mozzarella cheese
- ¼ cup grated Parmesan cheese
- 2 tablespoons of tomato paste
- 1 teaspoon of crushed red pepper flakes
- Salt and black pepper, to taste
- 1 ½ pounds chilled lean beef, cut into strips
- 1 pound chilled pork, cut into strips

Directions:

1. Preheat the oven to 350°F and line a rimmed baking sheet with foil. Set aside.
2. Assemble food grinder attachment by inserting the shaft into the hover and then place the blade. Use the large coarse grater and twist the ring on top to secure the parts in the food grinder.
3. Attach the food grinder attachment in the stand mixer power hub. Place a large bowl below the end of the grinder attachment and turn to "SPEED 4".
4. Add one slice of pork meat one at a time into the grinder and use the pusher to guide down the meat in the grinder. Continue the procedure with the remaining meat and repeat the procedure to grind

the meat twice. Transfer into a separate bowl. Repeat the procedure to grind the beef twice into the grinder attachment.

5. Replace food grinder attachment and set up the stand mixer with the flat beater. Add all ingredients for the meatballs in the mixer bowl together with the ground meat and mix on "STIR SPEED" until well incorporated.
6. Form the meat into small balls, stuff with a cube of cheese and roll to fully cover the cheese with meat mixture. Repeat procedure with the remaining ingredients.
7. Pour the oil in a deep pan, apply medium-high heat and wait until it reaches a temperature of 350°F. Fry the meatballs in two separate batches for about 1 to 2 minutes, or until lightly golden. Fry the remaining meatballs and transfer to the prepared baking sheets.
8. Bake it in the oven for about 10 to 15 minutes or until golden brown and cooked through. Remove from the oven, transfer the meatballs to a plate lined with paper towels and set aside to drain excess oil.
9. Transfer to a serving platter and serve warm with preferred dipping sauce.

JUICY STEAKHOUSE BURGERS

Create quality burgers by grinding your own meat. Chuck roast and flat iron steak are easy to find and are usually a good choice regarding the meat to fat ratio. This keeps the burgers from being too dry or too fatty.

Ingredients:

- 2 pieces of white bread, crusts trimmed and sliced into small cubes
- ¼ cup whole milk
- 2 ½ teaspoons of salt
- 1 teaspoon of crushed black pepper
- 1 tablespoon minced garlic
- 1 to 2 tablespoons of Worcestershire sauce
- 2 to 3 tablespoons of ketchup
- 2 pounds of chilled beef, sliced into strips
- 3 stems of green onions, minced
- Oil, for greasing

Preparation Time: 20 minutes
Cooking Time: 8 to 10 minutes
Yields: 8 patties

For Serving:

- 8 buns
- Sliced onions
- Lettuce
- Sliced tomatoes
- Condiments

Directions:

1. Assemble food grinder attachment by inserting the grind worm into the hover and then place the blade. Use the large coarse grater and twist the ring on top to secure the parts in the food grinder.
2. Attach the food grinder attachment in the stand mixer power hub. Place a large bowl below the end of the grinder attachment and turn to "SPEED 4".
3. Add one slice of beef at a time into the grinder and use the pusher to guide the meat into the grinder. Continue adding slices of meat in the food grinder and repeat the procedure to grind the meat twice.
4. Remove food grinder attachment and setup the stand mixer with a paddle attachment. Place the milk and cubed bread in the mixer bowl, allow to sit until bread has softened and beat on "STIR SPEED" until a paste mixture is achieved. Add the remaining ingredients together with the ground meat, except for the burger buns and condiments. Beat on "STIR SPEED" until well incorporated.
5. Preheat gas or charcoal grill and brush the grids with oil.
6. Remove the bowl from the stand mixer and divide the mixture into 8 equal portions. Shape into balls and lightly flatten to form into patties.
7. Reduce grill heat to medium-high and grill the burger patties for about 3 to 5 minutes on each side. Flip to cook the other side for another 3 to 4 minutes or cook further until the desired doneness is achieved.
8. Remove from grill, transfer to a plate and let rest for 5 minutes to allow the juices to penetrate back into the meat. Place one patty on each bun and top with desired condiments.

MARINARA SAUCE

if you are using your mixer to create your own pasta or even if you're not, making your own marinara is the surest way to up your cooking game. Once you make homemade sauce, you'll never want to go back to buying the grocery store jarred variety again. So much flavor! You can use any type of tomato, but roma tomatoes are known for producing the most flavorful sauce.

Ingredients:

Preparation Time: **20** *minutes*
Cooking Time: **1** *hour,* **30** *minutes*
Yields: **80** *ounces of sauce*

- 5 ½ pounds of red roma tomatoes
- 4 tablespoons of olive oil
- 12 ounces of tomato paste
- ½ cup of chicken stock
- ½ cup red wine
- 1 ½ tablespoons of minced garlic
- 1 large onion, diced
- 3 tablespoons of sugar
- 4 tablespoons dried parsley flakes
- 2 teaspoons dried oregano
- 3 teaspoons salt
- ½ teaspoon black pepper
- ½ teaspoon red pepper flakes
- 3 tablespoons of Italian seasoning mix
- 2 teaspoons dried basil

Directions:

1. Assemble strainer attachment by inserting the shaft and strainer into the hover of the food grinder. Place the cover knot on top and twist to secure the strainer in the food grinder. Place the straining cover over the strainer and place the strainer lid.
2. Attach the food grinder fitted with strainer attachment in the stand mixer power hub. Prepare two bowls for the strained ingredient and for the waste (seeds and skin).
3. Turn to "SPEED 6" and slowly add in the tomatoes in the food grinder.
4. While straining the tomatoes, sauté the garlic and onions in a large pot with oil for about 1 to 2 minutes. Season to taste with salt and pepper and stir in the rest of the ingredients together with the tomato juice.
5. Stir to combine and cook until it reaches a boil. Reduce to low heat and simmer for about 1 hour and 30 minutes while stirring occasionally. Adjust seasonings according to taste and serve over freshly cooked pasta.

GAZPACHO SOUP

Part drink, part soup, this recipe is great for those sweltering summer days when you just don't feel like eating. It's filled with nourishing vegetables, but still light enough to make a delicious lunch on a hot afternoon.

Ingredients:

- 1 pound of cherry tomatoes
- 1 cup diced seedless cucumber
- ½ cup diced red sweet pepper
- 1 medium red onion, diced
- 1 red jalapeno, seeded and finely chopped
- ½ teaspoon mince garlic
- 3 to 4 tablespoons of olive oil
- 1 organic lime, juiced
- 2 to 3 teaspoons of balsamic vinegar
- 2 to 3 teaspoons of Worcestershire sauce
- ½ teaspoon of ground cumin
- Salt and black pepper, to taste
- 2 tablespoons of fresh basil leaves chopped into strips

Preparation Time: 30 Minutes, Plus 2 Hours Of Chilling Time
Yields: 4 Servings

Directions:

1. Assemble strainer attachment by inserting the shaft and strainer into the hover of the food grinder. Place the cover knot on top and twist to secure the strainer in the food grinder. Place the straining cover over the strainer and place the strainer lid. Prepare two bowls for the strained ingredient and for the waste (seeds and skin).
2. Attach the food grinder attachment in the stand mixer power hub. Turn to "SPEED 6" and slowly add in the tomatoes in the food grinder. When all of the tomatoes are added into the strainer, transfer the tomato juice or puree in a separate bowl.
3. Mix together the remaining ingredients except for the basil and pass through the strainer until all ingredients are pureed. Combine tomato juice and the pureed ingredients and turn off the stand mixer to remove the food grinder attachment.
4. Adjust seasonings if desired and chill for at least 2 hours before serving. Portion the chilled Gazpacho into individual serving bowls and top with basil leaves before serving.

POMEGRANATE-CITRUS JUICE

This is a beautiful drink to serve and full of nutrients and healthy vitamins. While grapefruit can be a bit sour for some tastes, the other fruit juices help to mellow and sweeten the flavor. You can even mix it up and store it in a pitcher in the refrigerator if you don't drink it all at once.

Preparation Time: 10 minutes
Yields: 3 servings

Ingredients:

- 2 pomegranates, deseeded and halved
- 2 medium pink grapefruit, halved
- 2 medium oranges, halved
- 2 mandarins or tangerines, halved
- 1 small lime, halved
- Ice cubes, for serving

Directions:

1. Follow the steps from your stand mixer manual on how to assemble citrus juicer attachment. Attach juicer into the power hub and tighten the hub screw to secure the juicer. Place a bowl below the juicer and turn to "SPEED 6". Juice the pomegranates, remove the bowl and replace a new bowl below the juicer. Juice the rest of the citrus fruits and portion into 3 serving glasses, Fill the glasses with ice cubes and the juice from the oranges, grapefruit, tangerines and lime, and then pour the pomegranate juice on top and serve.

KEY LIME PIE

I love using the citrus juicer for many things, but one of my favorites is being able to use fresh key limes for my key lime pie. The bottled juice is fine in a pinch, but fresh key lime juice makes the pie so much better. Depending on how deep your pie plate is, you may have a little batter left over. If that's the case, I'll make 1 or 2 mini pies in a ramekin.

Preparation Time: 15 minutes, plus 1-2 hours for chilling
Cooking Time: 35minutes
Yields: 8 servings

Ingredients:

- 1 ½ cups of crushed graham crackers
- ½ cup sifted white sugar
- ¼ cup melted butter
- 2 ½ cups of canned, condensed milk
- 10 to 12 medium key limes, halved
- 1 tablespoon of key lime zest
- 2 large eggs
- 1 cup of reduced-fat sour cream
- 2 tablespoons sifted caster sugar

Directions:

1. Preheat the oven to 375°F and lightly grease a 9-inch pie plate with oil. Set aside.
2. Mix together the crushed graham crackers, sugar and butter in a mixing bowl until well combined. Transfer into the pie plate and press evenly on the bottom and sides to form the crust.
3. Bake for about 15 to 20 minutes, or until golden brown. Remove from the oven, let it rest to cool and reduce oven temperature to 325°F.
4. While baking the crust, prepare the filling. Follow the procedure in assembling your citrus juicer attachment and fit it into the power hub. Tighten the hub screw and place a bowl below the juicer. Turn to "SPEED 6" and juice all of the halved key limes.
5. Mix together the key lime juice, condensed milk and eggs using the paddle attachment for your stand mixer and pour into the prepared pie crust. Bake it in the oven for about 15 to 20 minutes, remove from the oven and chill for at least 1 to 2 hours when it has cooled.
6. While chilling the pie, whisk together the caster sugar and cream until smooth and spread evenly on top of the pie. Sprinkle with lime zest evenly on top and chill until slicing and serving.

HAM AND CHEESE SCALLOPED POTATOES

This is a great way to use up leftover ham after the holidays. Scalloped potatoes were always a hassle before I had a slicer for my stand mixer, but now they are quite easy. Potatoes are my favorite thing to slice using the Rotor Slicer, but I also love to use it to grate cheese and shred cabbage for coleslaw.

Preparation Time: 20 minutes
Cooking Time: 40-45 minutes
Yields: 6 servings

Ingredients:

- 3 tablespoons butter, divided
- 2 tablespoons of plain flour
- 1 ½ cups whole milk
- Salt and black pepper, to taste
- 1 cup thinly diced white onion
- 4 large Yukon gold potatoes, peeled
- 1-2 cups of baked ham, diced in small chunks
- ½ pound white Cheddar cheese, grated

Directions:

1. Preheat oven to 350 degrees. Butter a baking dish. In a saucepan, melt 2 tablespoons butter over medium high heat. Gradually add in the flour and cook until lightly brown.
2. Remove from heat and slowly pour in the milk while whisking constantly. Return to heat and cook until it reaches to a simmer while whisking regularly. Season to taste with salt and black pepper and remove from heat when it has thickened.
3. In a skillet, melt the remaining butter and sauté the onions until soft and tender. Stir in the ham and cook for about 2 to 3 minutes, or until lightly brown.
4. Insert the stand mixer's slicer/shredder housing into the power hub and tighten hub screw to secure attachment. Attach the thick slicing blade and shaft and insert into the housing.
5. Turn to "SPEED 6", place a wide bowl below the housing and add in one potato. Add another potato and continue until all of the potatoes are sliced.
6. Pour ¼ of the milk mixture in the prepared baking dish and spread evenly on the bottom. Layer half of the potatoes on top and spread half of the onion and ham mixture evenly on top. Cover with half of the remaining white sauce.Add the rest of the potatoes and top with the rest of the onion and ham mixture. Cover with white sauce and top with grated cheese.

7. Bake it in the oven for about 40 to 45 minutes, or until the edges are lightly golden and cheese has nicely melted on top. Remove from the oven and let it rest for about 10 minutes before slicing and serving.

GERMAN SAUSAGE (BRATWURST)

You will never have to buy pre-packaged Bratwursts again now that you have a sausage stuffer for your stand mixer. Use your food grinder to grind the meat and then use the stuffer to pack your casings. This particular recipe also makes delicious bratwurst burgers if you make the meat into patties instead of stuffing into the casings. Experiment with your favorite flavor of beer and enjoy the process of making your own brats!

Preparation Time: 3 ½ hours
Yields: 5 pounds

Ingredients:

- 3 pounds of chilled boneless pork butt, cut into strips or cubes
- 2 pounds of chilled lean beef, cut into cubes or strips
- 2 large eggs
- 1 cup of beer
- 1 teaspoon of crushed black peppercorns
- 1 teaspoon of smoked paprika
- 1 teaspoon chili powder or cayenne
- ½ teaspoon of ground nutmeg
- 1 tablespoon of prepared mustard
- 2 teaspoons of ground coriander
- 1 teaspoon of dried sage leaves, ground
- 4 teaspoons of salt
- 1 tablespoon of white sugar
- 2 teaspoons onion powder
- Hog casing

Directions:

1. Soak the casing in a bowl with water for about 30 minutes. Drain and set aside.
2. Assemble food grinder attachment by inserting the shaft into the hover and then place the blade. Use the large coarse grater and twist the ring on top to secure the parts in the food grinder.

3. Attach the food grinder attachment in the stand mixer power hub. Place a large bowl below the end of the grinder attachment and turn to "SPEED 4". Add in the pork meat slowly and lightly push to guide the meat into the grinder. Repeat the procedure to grind the meat twice and set aside the bowl.
4. Place another bowl below the food grinder and follow the procedure in grinding the pork. Turn off and setup the stand mixer with a beater attachment.
5. Add the egg, beer and set to "SPEED 2." Add the remaining ingredients into the mixer bowl and beat on "SPEED 4" until well combined. Add in the ground meat and beat further until well incorporated. Cover bowl and chill for at least 3 hours before stuffing.
6. Replace attachment with food grinder and set up the sausage stuffer by attaching the small nozzle. Rotate the cover knot and insert the hog casing into the nozzle. Tie the opposite end of the hog casing and slide the remainder into the nozzle.
7. Turn to "SPEED 4" and add the meat into the food grinder housing. Gradually add the meat and lightly press down to guide the meat into the grinder. While stuffing the casings, tie the casing every now and then when it has reached 5 to 6 inches long to form into links.
8. Cook immediately or store it in the freezer for future use.

GARLIC AND HERB SAUSAGE

This is a mild sausage with just a hint of spiciness that you can make with the Sausage Stuffer attachment. I love that I can use my mixer to help in every step of the process, from grinding to mixing and finally, stuffing the sausage.

Preparation Time: 2 hours
Yields: 3 ½ pounds

Ingredients:

- 2 teaspoons of crushed black peppercorns
- ½ teaspoon of crushed allspice berries
- 2 laurel leaves, torn into pieces
- 2 jalapeno peppers, seeded and chopped
- 2 pounds of chilled pork shoulder, cut into cubes
- 1 ½ pound of chilled (skinless and boneless) pork belly, cut into cubes
- ½ cup anisado or white wine
- 1 ½ to 2 tablespoons of salt
- 2 tablespoons of minced fresh oregano leaves
- 1 tablespoon of minced fresh lovage leaves
- Hog or sheep casing, for stuffing
- ½ head of garlic, peeled and pounded into paste

Directions:

1. Soak the casing in a bowl with water for about 30 minutes. Drain and set aside.
2. Assemble food grinder attachment by inserting the shaft into the hover and then place the blade. Use the large coarse grater and twist the ring on top to secure the parts in the food grinder.
3. Attach the food grinder attachment in the stand mixer power hub. Place a large bowl below the end of the grinder attachment and turn to "SPEED 4". Add the fat into the food grinder and regularly push down to guide the meat into the grinder. Remove bowl and replace with another one for the meat. Add in the pork meat slowly and lightly push to guide the meat into the grinder. Repeat the procedure to grind the meat twice and set aside the bowl.
4. Turn off mixer and setup the stand mixer with a beater attachment. Place the meat and fat into the mixer bowl together with the rest of the ingredients. Gradually turn to "SPEED 4" and beat until well combined. Remove the bowl from the mixer, cover and chill for a least 1 hours before stuffing.
5. Turn off stand mixer, replace attachment with food grinder and set up the sausage stuffer by attaching the small nozzle. Rotate the cover knot and insert the hog casing into the nozzle. Tie the opposite end of the hog casing and slide the remainder into the nozzle.
6. Turn to "SPEED 4" and stuff the casing until all of the meat has been used up. Tie the casing when it has reached 4 to 5 inches long while stuffing with sausage mixture to form into links. Turn off stand mixer, tie the end of the casing and cook immediately, if desired.
7. Or store it in the freezer for future use and consumption.

SPANISH CHORIZO

I love knowing exactly what is going into my food and by making my own chorizo with the Sausage Stuffer attachment, I can do just that. I can also control the level of spiciness depending on who I'm serving. Adjust the heat by adding more or less red and black pepper.

Ingredients:

Preparation Time: 2 hours
Yields: 12 links

- 2 pounds of chilled pork shoulder, cut into cubes
- ½ pound of chilled pork back fat, cut into cubes
- 1 tablespoons of minced garlic
- 2 ½ tablespoons of Spanish paprika
- 2 ½ to 3 teaspoons of salt
- 1 teaspoon of crushed red pepper flakes
- 1 teaspoon of crushed black peppercorns
- 2 tablespoons of anisado wine or dry white wine
- 1 hog casing

Directions:

1. Soak the casing in a bowl with water for about 30 minutes. Drain and set aside.
2. Assemble food grinder attachment by inserting the shaft into the hover and then place the blade. Use the large coarse grater and twist the ring on top to secure the parts in the food grinder.
3. Attach the food grinder attachment in the stand mixer power hub. Place a large bowl below the end of the grinder attachment and turn to "SPEED 4". Add the fat into the food grinder and regularly push down to guide the meat into the grinder. Remove bowl and replace with another one for the meat. Add in the pork meat slowly and lightly push to guide the meat into the grinder. Repeat the procedure to grind the meat twice and set aside the bowl.
4. Turn off mixer and setup the stand mixer with a beater attachment. Place the meat and fat into the mixer bowl together with the rest of the ingredients. Gradually turn to "SPEED 4" and beat until well combined. Remove the bowl from the mixer, cover and chill for a least 1 hour before stuffing.
5. Turn off stand mixer, replace attachment with food grinder and set up the sausage stuffer by attaching the small nozzle. Rotate the cover knot and insert the hog casing into the nozzle. Tie the opposite end of the hog casing and slide the remainder into the nozzle.
6. Turn to "SPEED 4" and stuff the casing until all of the meat has been used up. Tie the casing when it has reached 4 to 6 inches long while stuffing to form into links.
7. Cook immediately or store it in the freezer for future use.

COOKIES AND CREAM ICE CREAM

While I am more of a chocolate ice cream lover, my husband loves cookies and cream ice cream. I love to be able to experiment with different cookie types, Oreos, peanut butter, even homemade chocolate chip cookies.

Preparation Time: 10 Minutes
Freezing Time: 90 Minutes

Ingredients:

- 2 cups cooled, crumbled cookies (Oreos, NutterButters or any other cookie, crushed into bite-sized pieces)
- 1 ½ cups white sugar
- 1 ½ cups of whole milk
- 2 3/4 cups heavy cream
- 2 teaspoons vanilla

Directions:

1. Make sure your freezer is set at or below 0 degrees Fahrenheit (-18 degrees Celsius). Place the ice cream bowl attachment in the freezer for at least 15 hours.
2. Check that the ice cream bowl is completely frozen by giving it a shake before use. If you hear no movement, the bowl's cooling liquid are properly frozen.
3. Using your stand mixer and mixing bowl, use "SPEED 2" to mix the milk with the sugar until the sugar is fully dissolved.
4. Stir in the vanilla extract and the heavy cream, stirring thoroughly until all ingredients are evenly combined. Chill in the refrigerator for 1-2 hours.
5. Take the ice cream freezer bowl out of the freezer and set it on the middle of your stand mixer's base.
6. Slide the assembly drive onto the bottom of the mixer head. Fit the dasher into the bowl and connect to the assembly drive.
7. When your stand mixer is prepared, switch it into "STIR SPEED." The dasher will begin to turn in the bowl. Pour the refrigerated mixture immediately from the mixing bowl into the freezer bowl.
8. After approximately 20 minutes (in the last five minutes of freezing), add the crumbled cookie chunks into the ice cream bowl to let mix completely.
9. After approximately 25-30 minutes (total), the mixture will have frozen to a thick, creamy soft-serve consistency, with the crumbled cookies evenly distributed throughout. Serve directly from the ice cream freezer bowl into serving bowls or cones and enjoy!

LEMON SORBET

Classic lemon sorbet is the ultimate refreshing summer treat. Using your stand mixer ice cream maker attachment means you can make your own sorbet as well as all the memories that go with it, and isn't that the most fun? This frozen dish is the ideal palate cleanser or crisp frozen dessert that everyone loves.

Ingredients:

- 3 cups filtered water
- 3 cups white sugar
- 1 ½ tablespoons lemon zest
- 2 ¼ cups of freshly squeezed lemon juice

Preparation Time: 15 minutes
Freezing Time: 25 to 30 minutes

Directions:

1. Make sure your freezer is set at or below 0 degrees Fahrenheit (-18 degrees Celsius). Place the ice cream bowl attachment in the freezer for at least 15 hours.
2. Check that the ice cream bowl is completely frozen by giving it a shake before use. If you hear no movement, the bowl's cooling liquid is properly frozen.
3. In a large saucepan, mix the sugar and water and bring to a low boil over medium to high heat.
4. Lower the heat and continue to simmer the sugar and water, on low heat, without stirring, until the sugar has fully dissolved, about 3-5 minutes.
5. Remove from heat and allow to cool completely. This simple syrup can be pre-made and refrigerated ahead of time when making sorbet. Refrigerate until ready to move onto next steps.
6. Add the lemon juice and zest to the cooled syrup and stir to combine fully.
7. Take the ice cream freezer bowl out of the freezer and set it on the middle of your stand mixer's base.
8. Slide the assembly drive onto the bottom of the mixer head. Fit the dasher into the bowl and connect to the assembly drive.
9. When your stand mixer is prepared, switch it into "STIR SPEED." The dasher will begin to turn in the bowl. Pour the sorbet mixture immediately from the mixing bowl into the freezer bowl.
10. After approximately 25-30 minutes, the mixture will have frozen to a thick, soft icy consistency. Serve directly from the ice cream freezer bowl and enjoy!

CHOCOLATE ICE CREAM

For those who like their chocolate ice cream deep, dark, and rich as can be, this is the recipe for you. The custard like consistency of the base ensures that every spoonful of this ice cream is pure dense decadence. I particularly love the intensity of the Dutch cocoa in addition to the bittersweet chocolate. This ice cream is for serious chocolate lovers, so get ready to fall in love!

Preparation Time: 20 minutes
Freezing Time: 30 minutes

Ingredients:

- 2 ¼ cups whole milk
- 2 ¼ cups heavy cream
- 1 whole vanilla bean
- 1 1/8 cups white sugar
- 1 1/8 cups Dutch process chocolate cocoa
- 2 large eggs, whole
- 2 large egg yolks, (separated from whites)
- 12 ounces coarsely chopped bittersweet chocolate
- 2 teaspoons vanilla extract

Directions:

1. Make sure your freezer is set at or below 0 degrees Fahrenheit (-18 degrees Celsius). Place the ice cream bowl attachment in the freezer for at least 15 hours.
2. Check that the ice cream bowl is completely frozen by giving it a shake before use. If you hear no movement, the bowl's cooling liquid is properly frozen.
3. In a large saucepan, mix the whole milk and the heavy cream over a medium to low heat.
4. Using a sharp knife, split the vanilla bean down the middle lengthwise, then use the blunt end of the knife to scrape out the seeds of the bean.
5. Stir the seeds and the bean pod into the heating milk and cream mixture in the saucepan, and simmer on a low heat for approximately 30 minutes.
6. Extract the vanilla bean pod and discard it, and reduce the heat under the saucepan to the lowest setting.
7. Using your stand mixer and mixing bowl, beat or whisk the sugar, Dutch cocoa, whole eggs and egg yolks using "SPEED 8." Continue to beat or whisk until the mixture has thickened to a mayonnaise-like consistency.
8. Reduce the speed of the mixer to "SPEED 2." and add in one cup of the hot milk and cream mixture to the mixing bowl. Mix until evenly and smoothly blended.

9. Stir the chopped bittersweet chocolate into the remaining milk and cream mixture in the saucepan and stir continuously with a wooden spoon until the chocolate is melted and evenly blended in with the milk and cream mixture.
10. Add the egg mixture and continue to stir constantly over low heat until the mixture has thickened to a chocolate pudding like consistency.
11. Remove the saucepan from the heat and transfer the mixture to a large mixing bowl. Add in the vanilla extract and stir thoroughly until evenly combined.
12. Cover and refrigerate for at least 2 hours, until completely cooled.
13. Take the ice cream freezer bowl out of the freezer and set it on the middle of your stand mixer's base. Slide the assembly drive onto the bottom of the mixer head. Fit the dasher into the bowl and connect to the assembly drive.
14. When your stand mixer is prepared, switch it into "STIR SPEED." The dasher will begin to turn in the bowl. Pour the refrigerated mixture immediately from the mixing bowl into the freezer bowl.
15. After approximately 30 minutes, the mixture will have frozen to a dense, creamy soft-serve consistency. Serve directly from the ice cream freezer bowl into serving bowls or cones and enjoy!
16. For a more hard-frozen consistency, transfer the mixture from the freezer bowl into an air-tight container and keep in the freezer for at least 2 more hours.

BASIC PASTA DOUGH

Here is a recipe for basic pasta dough to use with any of the Pasta Attachments for the creation of your own homemade pasta. This dough will make pasta that is light and full of flavor. Each pound of pasta feeds 3-4 people, depending on serving size. Remember that fresh pasta will cook much faster than dried pasta.

Ingredients:

Preparation Time: 40 minutes
Yields: 3 to 4 Servings

- 4 eggs, beaten
- ¼ teaspoon fine salt
- 2 ½ cups all-purpose flour
- 1 tablespoon olive oil

Directions:

1. n the bowl that fits your stand mixer, whisk together flour and salt. Make a well in the flour.
2. Tilt motor head back and place the bowl securely on clamping plate. Insert flat beater onto the shaft, make sure that it is hooked properly and place lever on locking position to lock down the motor head completely.
3. Add the beaten eggs and olive oil into the well and turn mixer to "SPEED 2." Mixture should begin to form a stiff dough.
4. Switch the flat beater for the dough hook. Allow machine to knead for about 3-4 minutes.
5. Allow dough to rest for about 30 minutes before rolling out to desired thickness and using your choice of pasta roller.

FETTUCCINE ALFREDO

Fettuccine is one of my favorites. I love the rich creamy sauce and the big fettuccine noodles. Using your Pasta Roller and the Fettuccine cutter you can have fresh cut pasta in hardly any time at all.

Ingredients:

- 1 pound of pre-made pasta dough
- Extra flour, for dusting
- 2 ½ cups of heavy whipping cream
- 1 large lemon, juiced and zested
- ¾ cup of grass fed butter
- 2 cups of freshly grated Parmesan cheese
- 1 large pinch of ground nutmeg
- Salt and white pepper, to taste

Preparation Time: 40 minutes
Yields: 6 to 8 servings

Directions:

1. Work with a half-pound of pasta dough at a time to make it easier to handle. Lightly roll out each half before beginning to pass it through the pasta roller. Flour your work surface to prevent sticking.
2. Attach the pasta roller in the power hub and tighten screw to secure attachment. Adjust the roller to setting 1 to flatten the pasta sheet and turn to "SPEED 2 to 4". Pass the rolled pasta sheet into the roller and continue passing until smooth and flattened. Adjust the roller to setting 2 and pass the dough into the roller until thin and smooth. Adjust setting to 3 while passing the dough into the roller and readjust to setting 4 while repeating the procedure until a thin and smooth sheet is achieved. Remember to regularly dust the dough with flour while rolling to avoid sticking.
3. Adjust roller to setting 5. Pass the dough into the roller and make sure that the entire width of roller is filled with dough. Turn off stand mixer, remove roller and replace with the Fettuccine cutter.
4. Turn to "SPEED 2" and pass the flat sheet into the cutter. Catch the pasta that has been cut with one hand and slowly guide the remaining sheet into the cutter. Place the cut pasta on a baking sheet dusted lightly with semolina flour.
5. When the fettuccine pasta is done, turn off stand mixer and cook the pasta immediately in a pot with boiling water. Cook for about 3 to 4 minutes, or until al dente. Remove from the pot and drain completely.
6. In a medium skillet, apply medium-high heat and add in the 2 cups cream and butter. Cook until the butter has fully melted while stirring regularly. Do not boil. Remove the skillet from heat.
7. Stir in the remaining cream and Parmesan cheese. Toss to combine and add in the zest, nutmeg and season to taste with salt and white pepper. Toss with the cooked fettuccine noodles.
8. Portion into individual serving bowls, top with extra Parmesan and serve.

EASY FOUR CHEESE BAKED RAVIOLI

How rewarding is it to create your own ravioli? Well, set up your stand mixer with the ravioli maker and find out! If you've figured out the necessary steps to create your own pasta dough and roll it out, making ravioli is an easy next step. This is a simple but delicious mixed cheese filling but get creative and experiment with seasonal ingredients.

Preparation Time: 30 minutes
Cooking Time: 45 minutes
Yields: 9x13 baking pan

Ingredients:

- 1 pound of pasta dough
- 3 cups of jarred tomato and basil pasta sauce
- 1 cup of Mozzarella cheese, shredded
- 2 tablespoons of grated Parmesan cheese
- Oil, for greasing

For the Filling:

- 1 cup crumbled Ricotta cheese
- ½ cup softened cream cheese
- ½ cup grated Mozzarella cheese
- ½ cup grated Provolone cheese
- 1 large egg
- 1 ½ teaspoons mixed Italian herbs

Directions:

1. Mix together all filling ingredients in a mixing bowl until well combined. Set aside.
2. Roll out to flatten the pasta dough on a floured work surface.
3. Attach the pasta roller in the power hub and tighten screw to secure attachment. Adjust the roller to setting 1 to flatten the pasta sheet and turn to "SPEED 3". Pass the rolled pasta sheet into the roller and continue passing until smooth and flattened. Adjust the roller to setting 2 and pass the dough into the roller until thin and smooth. Adjust setting to 3 while passing the dough into the roller and readjust to setting 4 while repeating the procedure until a thin and smooth sheet is achieved. Remember to regularly dust the dough with flour while rolling to avoid sticking.

4. Adjust roller to setting 5. Pass the dough into the roller and make sure that the entire width of roller is filled with dough. Turn off stand mixer, remove roller and replace with the Ravioli maker. Lightly dust the pasta sheet with flour and fold the pasta sheet in half
5. Insert ravioli maker attachment and insert the folded side of the pasta sheet into the middle of the roller, draping the pasta sheet over each side of the rollers. Make sure to insert the center of the pasta sheet into the ravioli maker and twist the knob to feed the sheet into the ravioli maker.
6. Insert the hopper into the middle of the roller and press down until you hear it click into place. Scoop 1-2 scoops of filling into the hopper and spread evenly. Gently turn the knob to seal the filling into the raviolis and repeat the procedure with the remaining filling. Separate the ravioli by cutting along the line and set aside.
7. Preheat the oven to 350°F and lightly brush a 9x13 baking dish with oil.
8. Spread ½ cup of tomato sauce evenly on the bottom of the dish. Layer half of the ravioli on top of the sauce and cover with 1 ½ cups of sauce on top. Spread the mozzarella on top and layer the remaining ravioli over the cheese. Top with the rest of the tomato sauce. Finally, sprinkle with grated Parmesan.
9. Cover the baking dish with foil and bake it in the oven for about 40 to 45 minutes, or until bubbly and cooked through. Remove baking dish from the oven, let it rest for 10 minutes before serving.

EASY GARLIC SPAGHETTI

This is an easy recipe that highlights the delightful taste of freshly rolled pasta. Unlike dried pasta, homemade pasta is lighter and more delicate, but also more flavorful. Fresh pasta is best served with a light sauce to let the flavor of the pasta shine through. A stand mixer pasta press makes creating your own pasta incredibly simple.

Ingredients:

- 1 pound pasta dough (use recipe in the Pasta Roller section)
- 3 to 4 tablespoons of olive oil
- 1 tablespoon of minced garlic
- ½ teaspoon crushed red pepper flakes
- ½ teaspoon Italian seasoning mix
- Salt and pepper, to taste
- ¼ cup grated Parmesan cheese, for serving

Preparation Time: 15 minutes
Cooking Time: 15 minutes
Yields: 6 to 8 servings

Directions:

1. Insert the pasta press into the hub of your stand mixer and tighten screw to lock it into place. Select the spaghetti plate and insert into the ring and screw it onto the bottom of the pasta attachment.
2. Lightly dust the pasta dough with flour and form the dough into small balls, about the size of a golf ball.
3. Turn to "SPEED 10" and fill the housing with several of the dough balls. Use the combo tool if you need to push dough deeper into the unit. Catch spaghetti as it forms out of the bottom of the unit and cut at desired length. Place cut spaghetti on a lightly floured surface.
4. When all of the pasta dough has been used up, turn off stand mixer and disassemble the attachments.
5. Cook the spaghetti for about 3 to 4 minutes in a pot with boiling water. Remove from pot, reserve 1 cup cooking water and drain excess. Set aside.
6. Place the oil in a large skillet and apply medium-high heat. Sauté the garlic, crushed pepper and Italian seasoning for about 1 to 2 minutes, or until lightly golden.
7. Add drained pasta and 1 cup cooking water into skillet, season to taste with salt and pepper and cook until it has reduced a little bit while tossing regularly.
8. Portion into individual serving bowls, top with grated cheese and serve.

HOMEMADE ALL-PURPOSE FLOUR

Use the grain mill to grind your own all-purpose flour, which will take your baking to the next level. Freshly milled flour is healthy for you, as you know exactly what has gone into it. And there is just something tremendously satisfying about creating your own ingredients. Be sure not to mill too much, as freshly ground flour does not keep very well. One pound of wheat berries yields about 4 ½ cups of flour.

Preparation Time: 10 minutes
Yields: 4 ½ cups of flour per lb of wheat berries

Supplies Needed:

- 1 pound hard winter or hard red spring wheat berries

Directions:

1. Attach the grain mill attachment into the power hub and rotate the screw to secure attachment. Set up the grain miller to yield coarse grade flour and place the bowl below the housing. Turn to "SPEED 6", gradually add in the wheat berries and continue milling until all are used up.
2. Change the set up by using the finest grade of grain mill and pass the milled grain into the housing. When all of the grains are milled, turn off stand mixer.
3. Transfer the flour into a covered jar and store it in the pantry or in the fridge until used.

CPSIA information can be obtained
at www.ICGtesting.com
Printed in the USA
BVHW050955070119
537203BV00024B/1922